Framework

RE

3

Teacher's Resource

Joy White

Hodder Murray

A MEMBER OF THE HODDER HEADLINE GROUP

Hodder Murray
A MEMBER OF THE HODDER HEADLINE GROUP

Framework

RE

3

TEACHER'S RESOURCE

Joy White

Editor: John Keast

The publishers would like to thank the following for permission to reproduce copyright material:

Photo credits p.116 Barry Batchelor/PA/EMPICS.

Acknowledgements EMI (*My Sweet Lord*, Words and Music by George Harrison © 1970, reproduced by permission of Harrisongs Ltd/Peter Maurice Music Co Ltd, London WC2H 0QY); HarperCollins (quotation taken from *Heart of the Enlightened* © Anthony De Mello. Reprinted by permission of HarperCollins Publishers Ltd); Random House (extract from *An Evil Cradling* by Brian Keenan, published by Hutchinson. Reprinted by permission of The Random House Group Ltd).

The publishers would also like to thank the following:

Hodder (scripture quotations taken from the HOLY BIBLE, NEW INTERNATIONAL VERSION. Copyright © 1973, 1978, 1984 by International Bible Society. Used by permission of Hodder & Stoughton Publishers, A member of the Hodder Headline Group. All rights reserved. "NIV" is a registered trademark of International Bible Society. UK trademark number 1448790.); Poemhunter.com (*Heaven* © Steve Turner).

Every effort has been made to trace all copyright holders, but if any have been inadvertently overlooked the Publishers will be pleased to make the necessary arrangements at the first opportunity.

Although every effort has been made to ensure that website addresses are correct at time of going to press, Hodder Murray cannot be held responsible for the content of any website mentioned in this book. It is sometimes possible to find a relocated web page by typing in the address of the home page for a website in the URL window of your browser.

Orders: please contact Bookpoint Ltd, 130 Milton Park, Abingdon, Oxon OX14 4SB. Telephone: (44) 01235 827720. Fax: (44) 01235 400454. Lines are open 9.00 – 5.00, Monday to Saturday, with a 24-hour message answering service. Visit our website at www.hoddereducation.co.uk

© Joy White 2006
First published in 2006 by
Hodder Murray, an imprint of Hodder Education,
a member of the Hodder Headline Group
338 Euston Road
London NW1 3BH

Impression number   10 9 8 7 6 5 4 3 2 1
Year   2011   2010   2009   2008   2007   2006

Cover photo: Photograph of hands by John Lund/Corbis
Typeset in Formata Light 9/12pt by DC Graphic Design Limited, Swanley Village, Kent.
Internal illustrations by Clive Spong (Linden Artists) (cartoons) and Barking Dog Art
Printed by Hobbs the Printers, Totton, Hants.

A catalogue record for this title is available from the British Library

ISBN-10: 0340 90413 5
ISBN-13: 978 0340 904138

CONTENTS

Introduction   1

Unit 1: How does religion matter?   5
Introduction   5
1. Why do I need to know about religions?   8
2. What is the impact of religion in the world?   10
3. What impact can religion have on the individual?   13
4. How can a religion give purpose to life?   15
5. How might believers in the same religion differ?   17
6. What are people's rights regarding religion?   19
Worksheets   21

Unit 2: What is the impact of different religions on the community?   29
Introduction   29
1. Why are communities important?   32
2. Why do people help others in the community?   34
3. What roles do religions play in the community?   36
4. Why are there different types of schools?   38
5. Why do some religious communities live apart?   40
Worksheets   42

Unit 3: What insights do different religions bring to good and evil?   48
Introduction   48
1. How can people tell the difference between good and evil?   51
2. Why is there evil?   53
3. How is light used as a symbol?   54
4. How do we learn from our role models?   56
5. What attitudes do people have to heaven?   58
Worksheets   61

Unit 4: What do religions say about the use of money and other resources? 69

Introduction 69

1. What is the religious attitude to wealth? 72

2. What do religions say about ways of gaining wealth? 74

3. What about the earth's resources? 76

4. What do religions say about care for the environment? 78

5. What attitudes do religious people have to animals? 79

6. What makes us strong? 81

Worksheets 84

Unit 5: How do beliefs affect peace and conflict in the world today? 93

Introduction 93

1. Why are there conflicts? 96

2. Why are there different Christian attitudes to war? 98

3. How can peace be made and kept? 100

4. How can religions work together to create peace? 102

5. What attitudes do religions have to forgiveness? 104

6. When might conflict be necessary? 106

Worksheets 108

INTRODUCTION

Unit structure

Unit introduction

This sets out the purpose and contents of the unit, and includes a record of achievement sheet and a grid to identify the learning styles, skills and methods employed in each lesson.

Lesson plan

Aim

This gives a brief overall aim for each lesson.

Learning objectives

These are put in terms of knowledge and understanding for Attainment Target 1 (Learning about religion) and in terms of skills and attitudes for Attainment Target 2 (Learning from religion). This is not to say that skills are not found in AT1, or that there is not any knowledge and understanding in AT2 – the targets are interlinked. The learning objectives are derived from and directly related to the National Framework's Programme of Study for KS3, as shown in the matrix overleaf. Coverage of the learning objectives in this course will automatically cover the learning set out in the National Framework.

Skills and the use of ICT

These are separately set out to allow them to be identified with those required by the Key Stage 3 Strategy or any other requirement. Reference is also made at this stage to the *Framework RE 3 ICT Resource* that accompanies the Pupil's Book, and the Teacher's Notes that appear on the CD-ROM are given at the end of each lesson plan to show how they would fit within each lesson. The CD-ROM includes a starter, main and plenary activity for each lesson, which are designed as whole class activities to be used on a whiteboard.

Information

This section explains the nature and purpose of the Information section in the Pupil's Book. It covers specific background information relevant to that unit, and offers further information for your own use. It also explains how the information may be used in the lesson.

Activities

These are set out in the same order as the Pupil's Book, and are given in a logical sequence. They offer opportunity for various styles of learning and should provide plenty of work for pupils to do. How the activities may be differentiated is indicated, but teachers may want to vary their usage for different groups of pupils. An extension activity is always given, which is labelled as 'Now try this'. Each activity is marked with the attainment target it predominantly serves, though many activities are capable of being used for progress in both targets. Additional activities occasionally appear in the lesson plans and these are activities that could be included in lessons, but which have not been put into the Pupil's Book. They are provided to give greater flexibility to your teaching. Note that these are not necessarily extension activities.

Follow-up or homework

Suggestions here are to be used at your discretion, either to consolidate and reinforce learning or to prepare for the next lesson.

Assessment

By identifying the attainment targets that the activities predominantly relate to, assessment of progress in each target is simplified. You may assess pupils' work lesson by lesson by looking at their achievement in the activities undertaken, or choose one or more specific activities towards the end of the unit to assess pupils' progress overall. In Appendix A of each unit introduction, there is a chart listing all the activities and their targets for the whole unit. This can be used by pupils to track their own progress in a unit record of achievement, and help in the setting of targets for further improvement. It can also provide the basis for a teacher record of pupils' learning during each unit.

Curriculum link

Framework RE 3 follows on from, and builds upon, the themes covered in *Framework RE 1* and *2*. It is based on the KS3 Programme of Study in the new non-statutory National Framework for RE. This takes a new approach to the study of RE in schools, so this outline does not follow the pattern of previous RE courses and publications. It reflects the philosophical approach of the Framework and applies concepts of religious belief, practice and understanding to life and making ethical choices. To understand the nature of this course it is necessary to refer to the KS3 Programme of Study.

The following matrix links the book outline to the elements of the Programme of Study.

Framework RE 3	National Framework KS3 Programme of Study				
	(1) AT1 Learning	**(2) AT2 Learning**	**(3) Themes**	**(3) Religions**	**(3) Experiences and opportunities**
Throughout	1f vocabulary	2e expressing own beliefs	3h expressing spirituality	3a/b/c/d Christianity/ Buddhism/ Hinduism/ Islam/ Judaism/ Sikhism/ Religious community with local presence/ Secular	3m encountering people
Unit 1: How does religion matter?	1a analyse different impacts of religion on individuals	2b evaluate impacts of religion in the contemporary world	3a/j		3n/p/q visits, reflect on own beliefs, range of expression
Unit 2: What is the impact of different religions on the community?	1c explain why people belong to faith communities	2c reflect on the value of religion on human relationships	3e/f/j beliefs and concepts, authority, rights and responsibilities		3o/p/r discuss ultimate questions, reflect on own beliefs, explore connections
Unit 3: What insights do different religions bring to good and evil?	1e ultimate questions and ethical teachings	2c insights into value of religion	3e/f/l beliefs and concepts, authority, ethics and relationships		3o/p/q/r discuss ultimate questions, reflect on own beliefs, range of expression
Unit 4: What do religions say about the use of money and other resources?	1e ultimate questions and ethical teachings	2a/d relationships and ultimate questions	3h/k/l spirituality, global issues and interfaith dialogue		3m/o/p/q/r
Unit 5: How do beliefs affect peace and conflict in the world today?	1e ultimate questions and ethical teachings	2a/d evaluate own and others' beliefs	3j/k/l rights and responsibilities, global issues and interfaith dialogue		3m/o/p/q/r

The knowledge, skills and understanding that pupils will demonstrate in undertaking the activities are matched with levels 3 to 7 of the eight-level scales of the two attainment targets described in the National Framework for Religious Education.

How highly the pupils attain will depend on which activities they are asked to complete and how well they complete them. An assessment of this by the teacher (and the pupils also if self-, peer- or negotiated assessment is used) will determine their actual level of attainment. The pupils' attainments over time will provide evidence of achievement, and may be recorded on the Record of Achievement sheets included with each unit of the book. At the end of the term, year or key stage, these sheets will be a major factor in the summative assessment of each pupil's achievement for the purposes of self-evaluation, setting further targets, or reporting to parents.

Websites

As well as listing websites for each unit/lesson, a list of websites useful for this book is given here. It is not an exhaustive list, and many sites interlink. All the sites below lead to faith community's own websites. You should check websites out before suggesting them to pupils.

Name	Web address	Comments
RE online	www.reonline.org.uk	This site is a very useful portal for RE sites of many kinds, as well as advice and support for teaching and learning in RE, provided by the Culham Institute.
REXS	re-xs.ucsm.ac.uk	A long established and very useful site provided by St Martins College, Lancaster.
The RE site	allre.org.uk	Another very useful site with key words based on the QCA Glossary of terms, by key stages.
RE Directory	theredirectory.org.uk	An excellent RE directory of organisations, publishers, LEAs.
The RS Web	www.rsweb.org.uk	Access to religious studies of many kinds.
RE Net	education.cant.ac.uk/renet	Access to information and teacher issues, provided by Canterbury Christchurch University College.
BBC Religion	www.bbc.co.uk/religion	An excellent place for up-to-date information on religion and ethics.

LINKS BETWEEN FRAMEWORK RE and QCA SCHEME OF WORK DRAFT UNITS

The matrix on the following page shows how you will address the individual units in the non-statutory QCA Scheme of Work for Religious Education by following the Framework RE series. The units in each book have been ordered in a progressive way for sound pedagogical reasons, and by the end of the series you will have addressed each of the units in the non-statutory QCA scheme of work.

FW RE Units	1	2	3	4	5	6
Year 7	What is religion?	How and why are many people religious?	Where have the religions of the world come from and how are they linked?	What's so important about key religious figures?	What sort of attitudes result from being religious?	So what does being religious mean?
QCA Units	1; 3; 4	1; 4	2; 6	3; 6	1; 2; 4; 5	*
Year 8	Can religion be true?	How is religion true?	Where does the evidence come from?	How is religious authority used?	What does religion say about being human?	How does religion affect human behaviour?
QCA Units	1; 2; 3; 6	1	6	4; 5	4	3
Year 9	How does religion matter?	What is the impact of different religions on the community?	What insights do different religions bring to good and evil?	What do religions say about the use of money and other resources?	How does religion affect peace and conflict in the world today?	
QCA Units	5; 6	1	3; 5	2; 4; 5; 6	4	

* This unit is structured in such a way that work produced by the pupils can be used as a summative assessment of the whole year's work, and as such they pick up on the QCA units identified in Framework RE units 1–5 in the relevant year.

Key Stage 3 Attainment Targets

Learning about religion

1 Pupils should be taught to:

a investigate and explain the differing impacts of religious beliefs and teachings on individuals, communities and societies
b analyse and explain how religious beliefs and ideas are transmitted by people, texts and traditions
c investigate and explain why people belong to faith communities and explain the reasons for diversity in religion
d analyse and compare the evidence and arguments used when considering issues of truth in religion and philosophy
e discuss and evaluate how religious beliefs and teachings inform answers to ultimate questions and ethical issues
f apply a wide range of religious and philosophical vocabulary consistently and accurately, recognising both the power and limitations of language in expressing religious ideas and beliefs
g interpret and evaluate a range of sources, texts and authorities, from a variety of contexts
h interpret a variety of forms of religious and spiritual expression.

Learning from religion

2 Pupils should be taught to:

a reflect on the relationship between beliefs, teachings and ultimate questions, communicating their own ideas and using reasoned arguments
b evaluate the challenges and tensions of belonging to a religion and the impact of religion in the contemporary world, expressing their own ideas
c express insights into the significance and value of religion and other world-views on human relationships personally, locally and globally
d reflect and evaluate their own and others' beliefs about world issues such as peace and conflict, wealth and poverty and the importance of the environment, communicating their own ideas
e express their own beliefs and ideas, using a variety of forms of expression.

UNIT 1: HOW DOES RELIGION MATTER?

INTRODUCTION

The purpose of this unit is to consider the impact of religion on the individual, the community and the global world. The unit shows that it is immaterial whether someone is from a religious background or not as all are affected by the impact of religious beliefs. Case studies of a number of different religions are used to depict the range of religious and non-religious beliefs.

Contents

This unit consists of six lessons. It opens with a general exploration of the impact of religion – whether one is religious or not – and builds upon the first unit in the Year 7 Pupil's Book. This is followed by a lesson which explores how for some people their religion is a fixed point of reference, while a modern phenomenon is people changing religions or adopting non-religious life-stances. The third and fourth lessons contain case studies of the impact that a religious practice can have on a believer's lifestyle. The fifth lesson continues the theme of impact but it also investigates the diversity within the tradition. The final lesson provides an opportunity for pupils to understand the connection between practising a faith and human rights. This is a theme which is prominent throughout the book. All the case studies relate to the world of the pupils.

Appendices

- Appendix A: Record of achievement chart.
- Appendix B: Grid identifying the various learning styles, skills and methods employed in each lesson.

APPENDIX A

FRAMEWORK RE 3: RECORD OF ACHIEVEMENT
UNIT 1

PUPIL NAME: _____ GROUP: _____ TEACHER: _____

LESSON	AT1 Activity	AT1 Mark	AT2 Activity	AT2 Mark
1	1		
			2	
	3		3	
			NTT	
2	1		
			2	
			3	
			NTT	
3			1	
	2		
	NTT		NTT	
4			1	
	2		
	3		
			NTT	
5	1		
	2		
	3		
	4		
	NTT		NTT	
6			1	
	2		2	
			3	
			NTT	
LEVEL				

NOTES ON PROGRESS:

TARGETS:

Signed (Pupil) _____ Signed (Teacher) _____

APPENDIX B

UNIT 1: COVERAGE OF LEARNING ACTIVITIES, STYLES, METHODS, SKILLS

	Lesson 1	Lesson 2	Lesson 3	Lesson 4	Lesson 5	Lesson 6
Classification	✘					
Most likely				✘	✘	
Odd one out						
Reveal						
Sequencing			✘			
Show me						
Reflective questioning	✘		✘	✘		✘
Multiple choice				✘		
Ranking		✘	✘	✘		
Drag and drop		✘			✘	✘
Matching		✘	✘	✘		
Filling in gaps	✘				✘	
Writing	✘	✘	✘	✘	✘	✘
Brainstorming	✘	✘		✘		✘
Discussion	✘	✘	✘	✘	✘	✘
Comparing	✘			✘		✘
Investigating		✘		✘		✘
Questioning	✘		✘	✘	✘	
Explaining	✘		✘	✘	✘	✘
Giving accounts	✘					✘
Mind map	✘			✘		
Evaluating					✘	
Imagining		✘		✘		✘
Analysing			✘		✘	✘
Synthesising				✘		
Empathising	✘	✘	✘	✘		
Criticising						
Negotiating	✘	✘		✘	✘	
Deciding	✘	✘	✘	✘	✘	✘
Expressing clearly	✘	✘	✘	✘	✘	✘
Listening	✘	✘	✘	✘	✘	✘
Interpreting	✘	✘				✘
Applying	✘	✘				✘
Responding	✘	✘	✘	✘	✘	✘
Observing	✘	✘	✘			
Learning styles						
Kinaesthetic			✘			
Auditory					✘	
Visual	✘	✘	✘			✘

1. WHY DO I NEED TO KNOW ABOUT RELIGIONS?

Pupil's Book pages 2–5

Aim

The aim of this lesson is to make pupils aware that religion has a significant impact personally, locally and globally and that it is important to have a knowledge and understanding of religious traditions for the world of work.

Learning objectives

By the end of the lesson pupils should have:

- been able to recognise the differing impacts of religious beliefs on individuals, communities and societies (AT1a, 1f and 2c)
- recognised the importance of learning about religions for the world of work (AT2c)
- expressed insights into the challenges of belonging to a religion (AT2b).

Skills involved

Pupils will be:

- identifying the impact of religion on the individual, within the community and globally
- expressing ideas about possible challenges of belonging to a religion
- recognising the different careers that need a knowledge and understanding of religions.

Information

Within Britain there is a diminishing church attendance. The 2003 Mori Poll for the British Humanist Association found that although 37 million people in England and Wales said they were Christians, only 4 million people attended church each week.

The Seventh Day Adventists are Christians who believe in the imminent advent (Second Coming) of Christ. They were formally organised in 1863 and observe the Sabbath from sunset on Friday evening to Saturday evening as the day of rest, worship and ministry, in harmony with the teaching and practice of Jesus. It is a day of communion with God and one another.

Use of ICT

Research: To discover further examples of the impact of religion via the Internet. This could include looking at the day's newspapers on-line and identifying how many refer to a religious issue.

Communication: To record findings and communicate them to others. Activities 2 and 3 could be presented using ICT.

ICT Resource: See *Framework RE 3 ICT Resource* Teacher's Notes, page 9.

Activities

The activities are in a sequence and cover both AT1 and AT2.

The first two activities are intended for all pupils and provide an opportunity for diagnostic assessment as they require pupils to apply their previous knowledge and understanding. By working in pairs pupils will be able to support each other's application of past learning. Activity 3 is designed to stretch pupils and requires them to apply their knowledge and understanding and to make relevant suggestions.

Activity 1(AT1f)   Worksheet 1.1

The activity asks for two levels of understanding. For each picture (1–6) pupils are asked to select a caption to show the impact of a faith and then relate it to the specific example from each picture. By examining the pictures pupils will begin to interact with visual stimuli and so subsequently develop visual learning skills. The activity requires pupils to use appropriate religious vocabulary in writing captions for each picture. To support the needs of some pupils a basic word bank is given on Worksheet 1.1.

Expected responses:

Picture 1 – Many people wear something special to show
(a and ii)   they belong to a religious tradition, for example, many Sikh males will wear a turban.

Picture 2 – Many religions teach the importance of care
(e and v)   for animals, for example, Hindus show respect to the cow and will usually not eat beef.

Picture 3 – People of different religions send aid at times
(d and i)   of disaster, for example, Israeli aid is put together in Tel Aviv, to be sent to New Orleans to help people affected by Hurricane Katrina.

Picture 4 – Many religions have charities in Britain and
(c and iii)   overseas which work locally with people to help them, for example, Islamic Relief staff provide long- and short-term aid to displaced Sudanese people in an encampment in Western Dafur, Africa.

Picture 5 – Religions often give answers to important
(b and iv)   questions, like, 'What will happen when I die?', for example, many Christians believe that the soul goes to heaven.

Picture 6 – Some people consider it important to be
(f and vi)   educated in faith schools, for example, in many local communities pupils can attend Anglican and Catholic schools.

In Worksheet 1.1, pupils are asked to find two other pictures in the book which show the impact of religion. This gives an opportunity for pupils to use previous learning and a range of religious literacy in their explanation.

Class feedback will allow pupils to recognise that there are many common practices and traditions within religions. During the class feedback there will be opportunities for peer assessment as pupils can vote for the best captions for each picture. In the feedback it is important that pupils recognise the diversity of practice within religious traditions, for example, not all Sikhs wear a turban.

Activity 2 (AT2c)

In this activity it is important that pupils recognise that whether an answer is in the right column or not depends upon the strength of their justification. For example, Picture 6 has a significant impact on the individual who would attend such a school. It also has an impact on the community, as not all the community will attend such a school.

Activity 3 (AT1a and AT2c)

This activity is suitable for all pupils, although some may be helped by giving visual examples or through working in pairs. Answers may include:

What people eat – for example, caterer; nurse/doctor; air hostess; prison warden; member of the armed forces.

Which are the religious festivals – for example, any employer; jobs where people are expected to work on Saturdays or Sundays, such as people who work in the police force, transport industry, army, retail and media.

What happens when someone dies – any careers where people work with others, for example, teachers; social workers; undertakers; hospital staff; forensic scientist; florist.

Now try this (extension work) (AT 2b)

Pupils can then consider the career they are thinking of entering and the impact of knowing about religious traditions for themselves. If pupils are unaware of possible careers then a range of careers can be presented on different cards and pupils can discuss their decisions.

Suggestions for homework and follow-up work

The class can be split into groups to research different areas where religion may have an impact, for example, art and music; personal suffering; the home; treatment of animals. For each area the group is expected to research and find a range of examples of individual, local and global impacts. These can all be visually displayed on a notice board, which can change throughout the teaching of the unit. The displays should include positive and negative examples of the impact of religion.

Framework RE 3 ICT Resource Teacher's Notes

Starter activity

This activity is designed to show pupils the importance of religion within different types of media. It could act as a form of diagnostic assessment as it will reflect pupils' understanding of many issues, e.g. what is meant by a religious theme and what religion is being referred to. During feedback pupils can be challenged to consider if their choices have a religious theme or a secular theme in a religious context – for example, the film *Nuns on the Run* has a secular theme but it is based in a religious context (a nunnery), while the episode 'Homer the Heretic' in the *Simpsons* series has a religious theme.

Main activity

Pupils should be split into two teams to answer the question 'In which places or situations would someone be asked whether they follow a religion?' In turn, each team should give a different example in answer to the question. This can be done as a competition, where each team gets a point for a suggestion. It will support pupils in completing Activity 3 in the Pupil's Book (page 5).

Suggested answers

- in hospital
- in school
- at an undertakers
- in the armed services
- in prison
- when registering for marriage
- in a law court

Plenary activity

This activity requires pupils to look at three different problems connected with issues that may arise in the workplace or school because of someone's beliefs. Pupils are expected to answer the problems through empathising with the situation each individual finds themselves in and to offer practical solutions to the problem. If prompts are needed the 'go' button can be clicked on for suggested points for them to consider in their answers.

Each problem is on a separate screen. To move on to the next problem click on the arrow button at the bottom of the screen.

For problem 1 it is not expected that pupils will have a working knowledge of Seventh Day Adventism and you could give some background information, explaining that it is a Christian denomination and that their Sabbath is from Friday sunset to Saturday sunset. They believe the Creator rested on the Seventh Day and gave the Sabbath as a memorial of creation. For this reason they should avoid any form of work on a Saturday. For this problem pupils are expected to make their own personal views as to when the employer should be told and also to give an informed range of suggestions. Their considerations might include whether the person should turn down the job, explain to their prospective employer about their religion before accepting the job, or wait until they are in the job to explain.

For problem 2 pupils should be aware of the importance of the kippah for some Jews from previous learning. Some pupils may refer to it as a yarmulke. Orthodox Jewish males usually wear it all the time. For this problem pupils are expected to make their own personal view as to whether it should be worn at school or not.

For problem 3 pupils should be aware of the difference between praying in an assembly and listening to moral stories from sacred texts or notices about school life. The distinction should be made about the different aims of collective worship in a school and RE.

For all the problems pupils should be aware of the challenges of 'standing out' from the rest within a formal structure such as a school or workplace.

2. WHAT IS THE IMPACT OF RELIGION IN THE WORLD?

Pupil's Book pages 6–9

Aim
The aim of this lesson is to raise pupil's awareness of the significance of religion on contemporary issues.

Learning objectives
By the end of the lesson pupils should have:
- found features of religion in the local community (AT2c)
- investigated the effect of religion on contemporary issues (AT1a and 2b)
- given an opinion concerning an event of religious significance (AT2b and 2c).

Skills involved
Pupils will be:
- finding features of religion in the local community
- investigating the impact of religion on current issues
- evaluating the challenges and tensions of belonging to a religion.

Information
There is no information section as such in this lesson. Pupils investigate the impact of religion throughout the range of stimuli. All the materials and activities of the lesson will be reinforced by a knowledge of religion within the local community. This could be supported by the classroom display produced from the homework activity for Lesson One. If it is impossible to produce a class display then pupils could make a group collage, which could be used during the lesson.

Use of ICT
Research: To find more examples of newspaper headlines and articles which are related to religion.
ICT Resource: See *Framework RE 3 ICT Resource* Teacher's Notes, page 11.

Activity 1 (AT1a)
This activity builds on learning from *Framework RE 2* and supports diagnostic assessment. It should encourage pupils to critically investigate and interpret pictures. By working in pairs pupils will need to explain their findings using a range of religious terms and to listen to each other.

Once pupils have been given an opportunity to report their findings, a range of differentiated key words could act as prompts. These could include:

- Christian
- Buddhist
- Mosque
- Muslim
- Islam
- Church
- Halal
- Charity
- Hijab.

Activity 2 (AT2b)   Worksheet 1.2

In this activity pupils will be expected to hypothesise what main features or points of information could be contained within articles related to certain newspaper headlines. The choice of headlines is differentiated to support and extend the range of abilities within a class. Pupils may be directed to the titles which are most suitable for their level or to work with a partner who will be able extend their understanding. Worksheet 1.2 will support accessibility and extension as it contains a range of different background materials which would contextualise the headlines.

Pupils should be encouraged to show the implications of each of the headlines, for example, a consideration of 'Church helps local refugee family' could include:

- why a refugee family may need help
- what a church community could do
- how these actions would reflect the teachings of Jesus
- the example this may set to the community
- the role of the church leaders.

Activity 3 (AT2b)

In this activity pupils need to express their understanding as to why some Christians may consider the use of the statue to be blasphemous and offensive. The activity does not ask for the pupil's views on the issue but to be able to explain the issue.

Now try this (extension work) (AT2b)

More able pupils can be asked to respond to the statement. They should be able to give a justification for their response.

Suggestions for homework and follow-up work

1 Ask pupils to find a local newspaper cutting, picture or leaflet which shows how religion affects current issues. Newspaper cuttings can be added to the wall display created in the first lesson or can be used to create a collage.
2 Pupils will need to explain why what they have found is a religious issue.

Framework RE 3 ICT Resource Teacher's Notes

Starter activity

Pupils are expected to write labels for different parts of the picture. For each label they need to identify what each part of the picture shows and then explain how it is connected to religious beliefs. The activity is intended to remind pupils of previous learning.

Further information is provided by clicking on 'suggested answers'. This can then be used in the investigation in Activity One in the Pupil's Book (page 6). Pupils should read out the key words and definitions (page 8) to support their religious literacy. There are eight things to identify, one on each screen. Click on the arrow at the bottom of the screen to go to the next.

Suggested answers

1 Mosque – place of worship for Muslims. Many mosques also have a madrassah where Muslims learn to read and recite the Qur'an.

2 Church – place of worship for Christians. There are many different types of church buildings that reflect different denomination. This is an Anglican church.

3 Halal butcher – sells meat that has been prepared according to Muslim food laws. 'Halal' means allowed.

4 Christian Aid – a Christian charity that provides emergency aid and supports long-term development projects.

5 Buddhist monk – dedicates his life to practising the dharma.

6 Buddhist Centre – a place for Buddhists to meet.

7 Hijab – head covering often worn by Muslim women.

8 Salvation Army – Christian denomination that does charitable works.

Main activity

This activity will support Activity Two in the Pupil's Book (page 7). Each of the six headlines is displayed on a separate screen with a selection of words. Pupils should identify three words they could use in an article accompanying each headline by dragging and dropping the words into place and then giving justifications for their choices. The words are differentiated and should help prompt pupils' responses. Some justifications for answers will be obvious, for example Sikhs worship in a gurdwara and therefore would be linked with headline 3. Some answers will require deeper thought and more advanced thinking skills, for example how free will could relate to all of the headlines.

To move onto the next headline, or back to a previous one, use the arrow buttons at the bottom of the screen.

Suggested answers

Key terms	Article 1	Article 2	Article 3	Article 4	Article 5	Article 6
Muslim	X					
Sikh			X			
Jesus			X		X	X
Qur'an	X					
Parable of the Good Samaritan					X	
Church of England			X			X
Defender of Faiths			X			
Inter-faith dialogue			X		X	X
Natural family planning		X				
Roman Catholics		X				X
Fit or proper				X		
Free will	X	X	X	X	X	X
Leviticus				X		

Plenary activity

The activity asks pupils to consider the impact of religion around them. They are expected to put in order the impact of various actions on the local community – from most positive at the top, to least positive at the bottom – giving justifications for their choices. There is no correct order; the idea is to provoke discussion about the effect or intrusion of religion. Certain considerations may include:

- the difference between dialogue and evangelism

- implications of actions, for example by visiting different places of worship you may be creating inter-faith dialogue within the community

- the good or harm each action can have, for example some people might consider going from door to door is an intrusion and some might be grateful to learn about other religions.

3. WHAT IMPACT CAN RELIGION HAVE ON THE INDIVIDUAL?

Pupil's Book pages 10–13

Aim

The aim of this lesson is to teach pupils that religion can have a role in forming an individual's identity and life experiences.

Learning objectives

By the end of the lesson pupils should have:

- expressed their own beliefs and ideas using a variety of forms of expression (AT2e)
- reinforced their knowledge and understanding of the role religion can play throughout an individual's life (AT1a)
- considered key factors of their own identity (AT2c).

Skills involved

Pupils will be:

- reflecting upon the different features of their own identity
- recognising that religion is an important part of many people's identities
- investigating the impact of belonging to a religion for the individual
- recognising the role of free will and free choice.

Information

Twins Amrit and Rabindra Singh are British artists who combine western and eastern art practices. On their first visit to India in 1980 they were fascinated with Mughal minature paintings. Within each painting there will be a range of different symbolism used. The picture *All That I Am* depicts the holiest Sikh site – the Golden Temple at Amritsar. This was originally built by Guru Arjan in 1588. The temple has four doors to show that people from all directions are welcome. Inside are three copies of the Guru Granth Sahib.

Use of ICT

Research: To find more pictures by the Singh twins and identify the role of their beliefs and religious tradition. Pupils could use the following web address to research further pictures by the Singh twins: www.singhtwins.co.uk.
Communication: To record and present findings. In Activity 1, nstead of writing down influences, pupils could record their reflections in visual form.

ICT resource: See *Framework RE 3 ICT Resource Teacher's Notes*, page 14.

Activity 1 (AT2e)

This activity is based on the picture *All That I Am* by Amrit KD Kaur Singh. Pupils are expected to investigate the picture and apply past knowledge and understanding to interpreting it. They should be able to draw on their previous learning of Sikhism. Some pupils may need prompts to consider what is happening in each of the images. The picture shows:

- her father's birth in India
- the Golden Temple at Amritsar (the holy temple for Sikhs)
- the importance of Ghandi and the blood that was spilt during the partition in India
- his journey to England where he has a relatively poor background
- the first film he sees that makes an impact
- his job as a door-to-door salesman
- his struggle to get an education and eventually to study medicine
- the purchase of a new house.

Interspersed throughout the events are the reminders of his religious and cultural roots, such as the representation that he is still wearing the turban; the prayer book; the family photograph. An outcome should be that pupils recognise the role that beliefs, values, traditions and sometimes the experiences that come from those three things have on an identity. For the artist it is also an acknowledgement that she is a product of the life experiences, sacrifices and achievements passed onto her by her father.

In the second part of the activity pupils should reflect on their own values and experiences which have helped form their identity.

Activity 2 (AT1a)

In this activity there are seven pictures showing different impacts of religion on the individual and pupils have to match captions with the appropriate pictures. To support pupils' religious literacy, opportunities should be given for pupils to speak and write the captions. It is intended that pupils use their previous learning on Islam to support the activity.

The correct answers are:

Picture 5: Whispering the adhan into Adel's ear when he is born to welcome him into the Ummah.

Picture 6: Celebrating Id-ul-Fitr.

Picture 1: Learning the whole of the Qur'an by heart to become a hafiz.

Picture 3: Being wrapped in white and circumcised (Khitan) to fulfill the command of Allah to the prophet Ibrahim.

Picture 2: Deciding whether to eat halal (allowed) food.
Picture 4: Deciding who to marry.
Picture 7: Considering the big questions of life such as why do people suffer? What happens after you die?

This activity can also be carried out by using the main ICT activity on Framework RE 3 ICT Resource where pupils can drag and drop the correct captions into place.

In the second part of the activity, pupils requiring a further challenge can sequence the pictures of Adel's life. This should challenge pupils to consider what might be 'fixed' landmarks in traditions and when individual choices might be made. This should show how there may be many different practices within one religious tradition.

Discuss with pupils the reasons for the variances. There will be particular differences concerning when decisions regarding marriage may be made. Some pupils may also refer to the difference depending upon the cultural traditions of the country where Adel lives. For example the khitan ceremony in Turkey often doesn't take place until a boy has reached the age of nine.

In the final part of the activity pupils have to consider what would have an influence on the different features of Adel's life. A range of different categories are provided and pupils should recognise that specific influences will often relate to the chronological order they have decided on.

Now try this (extension work) (AT2c and AT2e)

This statement by Rabbi Sachs was written when he was referring to how devastating the condition of Alzheimer's is, which robs people of their memories. Pupils will be expected to consider what has been passed onto them and what they would want to pass onto a future generation.

Suggestions for homework and follow-up work

Worksheet 1.3

1 Pupil's could use the picture of *All That I Am* as a model to create someone close to them.
2 By using the template on Worksheet 1.3 pupils can reflect on the main parts of their identity and what or who has had the most influence on them. They can record their findings either as illustrations or in a symbolic collage.

Framework RE 3 ICT Resource Teacher's Notes

Starter activity

This activity asks pupils about their own thoughts on the importance of religion to identity by getting them to classify a range of characteristics about themselves into whether they are very important, important or not important when describing themselves to someone else. The idea is to provoke discussion about the importance of different aspects of identity. The activity is based on research which found that many people – especially Hindus and Muslims – felt their religion would tell a stranger more about them than any of their other characteristics.

Main activity

In this activity pupils are asked to rearrange the events in a Muslim's life into the order they think they would happen. This supports Activity Two in the Pupil's Book (page 12). There is no correct answer but some of the events must be placed in a certain order:

1 Having the Adhan whispered in his ear.

2 Being circumcised (Khitan).

The other events may occur at different times depending upon the individual and their faith journey, for example becoming a hafiz, making decisions about whether to use contraceptives or whether to eat halal food. There are also some events that might re-occur at different times, for example celebrating Id-ul-Fitr would be an annual event, or thinking about the big questions of life may happen at several times during Adel's life.

The purpose of the activity is to encourage discussion about the fixed points in a believer's life and the many different times when a believer makes a choice to follow the teachings of their religion. The activity also shows the impact of faith and belief on an individual's life.

Plenary activity

This activity supports the development of emotional literacy. It provides an opportunity for stilling as pupils reflect upon what makes them unique. Pupils can write their response on a label and give it to the teacher as they leave. These can then be collated and used to show the talents of the whole class.

4. HOW CAN A RELIGION GIVE PURPOSE TO LIFE?

Pupil's Book pages 14–17

Aim

The aim of the lesson is for pupils to reflect upon the purpose of life and recognise that for some people their lives are directed by their faith.

Learning objectives

By the end of the lesson pupils should have:
- considered how they would like to be remembered in their lives/the purpose of their lives (AT2e)
- recognised the importance of religious beliefs in some people's lives (AT1a)
- interpreted a form of spiritual expression (AT1h).

Skills involved

Pupils will be:
- reflecting upon their own views concerning the purpose of life
- interpreting a form of spiritual expression
- investigating the impact of religious beliefs through a life story.

Information

The life of Muhammad Ali can be used to illustrate many aspects of Religious Education. In addition to his decision to become a conscientious objector he has also committed a great deal of his time and energy to fundraising and charity appeals. Muhammad Ali is also an example of someone who adopted a different religious tradition during his life. When discussing his religious beliefs it is important that pupils are aware that people who become Muslims are known as reverts rather than converts.

Although the focus of Matthew Archer's work (pages 16–17 of the Pupil's Book) is in Brazil it is important to show the wider context of street children within the world. It is estimated that there are up to 170 million children who live 'on the streets' throughout the world. Research through the various websites will develop an awareness of the global situation. In Brazil there are up to 30 million street children who face violence and killings every day. There is a National Movement of Street Boys and Girls which tries to demand rights and respect.

Use of ICT

Research: Pupils can use a range of relevant websites to help them complete Worksheet 1.4:
www.streetchildren.org.uk
www.mnmmr.org.br
www.whiteband.org
www.makepovertyhistory.org
www.mkarcher.com.

Communication: Pupils can present their concept map in Activity 3 using ICT. The leaflet in the homework task can be produced using ICT.

ICT Resource: See *Framework RE 3 ICT Resource Teacher's Notes*, page 16.

Activity 1 (AT2e)

Pupils are expected to consider what would give them most purpose in life. The rank ordering will be individual but it would be appropriate to introduce the concept of utilitarianism – the greatest happiness for the greatest number. The second part of the activity may include a discussion concerning how people who have died young may have fulfilled a purpose for which they are still remembered, for example, Anne Frank.

Activity 2 (AT1a and AT1h)

This activity requires pupils to identify key concepts expressed in the poem, for example, being a trustee; life as a test; impermanence; materialism; eternal life, and to consider the impact of these views on daily life. If possible, extracts from the film on Muhammad Ali could be shown to relate these beliefs to particular instances in Muhammad Ali's life.

Activity 3 (AT1a) Worksheet 1.4

To complete this activity pupils will need to read the interview to be able to identify key concepts and examples. Worksheet 1.4 will allow pupils to highlight examples of each concept in the dialogue before they try to construct their concept map. Answers may refer to:

Vocation – loss of status as a teacher/lack of material goods, etc.

Service – to God/to the worshipping community in England/to the community in Brazil, etc.

Faith – going to a new country/believing in the goodness of people in a new country/relying on charity, etc.

Courage – leaving the life you know/moving to a different country/dealing with violence, etc.

In the second part of the activity pupils can work in pairs to decide the type of question that might have resulted in this response. Highlighting key words may help some pupils focus on relevant questions. Many responses will include the concept of vocation or purpose of life.

The questions the pupils come up with for the final part of the activity will help assess pupils' understanding of vocation and purpose. To support this activity the teacher could model appropriate and inappropriate questions, for example:

Is it very hot in Brazil?
Do you think God will protect you from violence?
Why do you think God selected you?

Now try this (extension work) (AT2e)

Support may be given through a bank of key words to use, for example, purpose; career; money; calling; service. This activity requires pupils to teach each other the key concept of vocation. Research shows that teaching others is the most proficient way of learning.

Suggestions for homework and follow-up work

Worksheet 1.5

1 Use websites to produce a charity leaflet showing why people should support the rights of street children across the world.
2 Completing Worksheet 1.5 will support pupils' awareness of the situation of the street children and the role of charities.

Framework RE 3 ICT Resource Teacher's Notes

Starter activity

In this activity pupils will be introduced to people who have had a purpose in life and have had a marked effect on society through their strength of character. Pupils should flip over a card from each row to see if the person, name and description match. When they match the cards will disappear from the screen when 'go' is clicked on. A discussion about each individual's characteristics and their effect on society could then take place.

Answers

1 Martin Luther King. American Baptist Minister who led the Black civil rights movement and was awarded the Nobel Peace Prize.
2 Anne Frank. Jewish girl who wrote a diary while in hiding in Amsterdam during World War II.
3 Ellen MacArthur. Sailed solo around the world in the fastest time.
4 Mother Teresa. Served the diseased and dying on the streets of Calcutta and was awarded the Nobel Peace Prize.

Main activity

Pupils should work on their own to write a postcard to a friend. They should imagine they are visiting Open House in Brazil (as described in the Pupil's Book pages 16–17). In order to decide what to write on their postcard they should consider what they might see at Open House and also the effect of the work of Open House on the children they meet.

Plenary activity

Pupils should work in small groups to decide the best points to be used in a summary of the main learning points from the lesson. Each group should then provide a summary point to complete the boxes.

Suggested answers
The main points might include reference to the following:

- The purpose of life – most people want their life to count.
- Martin Luther King refers to the importance of having a meaning or purpose to life.
- Some people, such as Muhammad Ali, would consider the way they live their life to be a test of faith.
- Christians believe that God has a purpose for everyone and that they may be called to do special work for God (vocation).
- The work of Matthew Archer is an example of Christian vocation and faith.
- The work that Open House does, shows Christian beliefs about helping others in practice.

5. HOW MIGHT BELIEVERS IN THE SAME RELIGION DIFFER?

Pupil's Book pages 18–21

Aim

The aim of the lesson is to teach pupils that people from the same religion may have different beliefs and practices.

Learning objectives

By the end of the lesson pupils should have:
- recognised that beliefs have different impacts upon people (AT1a)
- investigated why believers in the same religion may have different practices (AT1b and 1c)
- understood the difference between religion and nationality (AT1c)
- distinguished between some of the practices of Orthodox and Reform Jews (AT1b and 1c).

Skills involved

Pupils will be:
- investigating why believers in the same religion may have different practices
- distinguishing between some of the distinctive practices of Orthodox and Reform Jews
- understanding the difference between religion and nationality.

Information

The term 'kosher' means fit or proper. In Leviticus Chapter 11 there are lists of animals, birds and fish, which can and cannot be eaten.

Animals and fish that can be eaten include any that are cloven footed and chew the cud or have fins such as cow, ox, sheep, goat, chicken and many types of fish. Those that can't be eaten include pig, horse, hare, and shellfish.

Under kosher regulations meat and milk should not be eaten at the same meal.

The preparation, cooking and washing up of meat and dairy are all kept separate. The ideal is to have two sets of utensils and crockery. All meat has to be drained. It is salted and soaked in water to remove the blood.

All Jews share much in common, including a shared history, but there are differences of traditions and beliefs. Most Jewish families will have members affiliated to a variety of branches of Judaism.

The main difference between Orthodox and Reform Jews concerns the Torah. Orthodox Jews believe that God dictated it to Moses and therefore it is the ultimate authority for a Jewish way of life. Reform Judaism says the Torah was divinely inspired but that Judaism is a living religion which should move with the times.

Use of ICT

Research: To use the Internet to find further information on kosher diets or kashrut and to answer Activity 3 and Worksheet 1.6. The following websites are a good starting point:
www.kashrus.org
www.kosher.org.uk.

Communication: The Venn diagram in Activity 2 can be presented electronically.

ICT Resource: See *Framework RE 3 ICT Resource* Teacher's Notes, page 18.

Activity 1 (AT1a)

This activity should make pupils aware that despite a group having a general bonding or connection, people within it will have a range of different attitudes and practices. The use of all/some/many/few should be encouraged when pupils are referring to people's beliefs, values and practices. This is reinforced through the Plenary Activity on the *Framework RE 3 ICT Resource*.

Activity 2 (AT1b and AT1c)

In this activity pupils identify distinguishing practices. Answers may include:
- Orthodox:
Follow rules of the Torah.
Keep all the laws of kosher.
Must eat where food laws are kept.
- Both:
Believe in God.
Consider the Torah special.
Celebrate Shabbat.
- Reform:
Shabbat is very special but can use modern technology.
Will keep some forms of kosher.

Activity 3 (AT1b and AT1c)

This activity requires pupils to plan how they will gain the necessary information for the arrival of a Jewish person who eats kosher food. They should be able to cite specific resources and websites (see those suggested above).

In the second part of the activity, pupils need to consider what is the most reliable source of evidence. In their justifications, pupils may consider the validity of the author; the intention of the source of evidence; whether the source of evidence reflects the contemporary situation, etc.

Activity 4 (AT1c)

This activity requires pupils to understand the teachings in the dialogue and also to feel empowered to correct misconceptions. Answers may include:
a) All Jews may have the same history/Jews have different practices/even within a family there will be different practices/a Jew's beliefs may derive from their family tradition, area of origin, free will, life experiences.

b) Jews will reflect their country of origin/they may be converts.

c) What is a 'true' Jew? Most Jews will eat some form of kosher but there are many different rules that people may follow. Some Orthodox Jews may consider this statement to be true.

d) Judaism is the religion, India is the country – you can be both. Judaism has spread throughout the world.

e) There is no such thing as Jewish food, but there are types of food that many Jews eat because of the laws of kashrut or kosher and their country of origin.

Now try this (extension work) (AT1a)

This activity requires pupils to analyse the information and to summarise a key point for and against a statement of belief. Arguments might include:

I agree because …

- religious rules are for eternity
- following the rules shows you are a member of that faith
- the only reason you would change a rule is because it's easier and that's not what being religious is about.

I disagree because …

- people have to be individuals and interpret things in their own way
- it's the central beliefs that are most important
- for some people it may be impractical for them to follow all the rules and then they may feel they have to leave the religion.

Suggestions for homework and follow-up work

Worksheet 1.6

1 Worksheet 1.6 requires pupils to identify different types of Jews and particular traditions and practices. Pupils should become aware of the breadth and diversity of the tradition.

Expected answers would be:

- Nathan – Orthodox Jew.
- Beckie – Ashkenazi Progressive Jew.
- Leah – Secular Jew.

2 Find some pictures using the Internet to show how Judaism is a worldwide religion with many different practices.

Framework RE 3 ICT Resource Teacher's Notes

Starter activity

This activity gives an opportunity for a diagnostic assessment which challenges stereotypical preconceptions. Pupils look at a series of pictures of people and have to guess what they have in common after each picture is revealed. Pupils should make a suggestion after each picture, which will either change the preceding suggestion or affirm it. There will be an opportunity for a discussion concerning secular and religious groups and also about the differences between religion and race and culture. For some classes it would be appropriate to introduce the distinction between Ashkenazi (Jews who settled in France, Germany, Poland and eastern Europe), Sephardic (Jews of Spanish and North African origin) and Falasha Jews (Jews from Ethiopia). If pupils answer correctly from the first clues, finish showing the rest before opening the discussion.

Answer

They are all Jewish/belong to the Jewish tradition.

Main activity

In this activity pupils are expected to apply their learning from Activity One in the Pupil's Book (page 18) and the dialogue between Jo and Leah in the Pupil's Book (page 19). They should decide whether 'some', 'many' or 'all' should be the word at the start of each sentence and drag and drop their choice into place.

Answers

1 All Jews have a shared history.

2 Many Jews are considered Orthodox.

3 Some Jews are called secular and do not believe that religion has a large part in their life.

4 Many Jews follow kosher practices within their homes.

5 Some Jews live in India and China.

6 Some Jews live in Israel.

Plenary activity

In this activity you could organise the pupils into teams to compete to solve the anagrams first. During feedback, in addition to solving the anagram, you could ask them to give a definition of each word. It is important for pupils to pronounce each of the words as this will support development of their religious literacy.

Answers

1 Culture	4 Stereotype
2 Orthodox Jews	5 Shabbat
3 Kosher	

6. WHAT ARE PEOPLE'S RIGHTS REGARDING RELIGION?

Pupil's Book pages 22–25

Aim

The aim of this lesson is to teach pupils that belonging to a religion can present many challenges.

Learning objectives

By the end of the lesson pupils should have:
- thought about the effects of prejudice and discrimination (AT1g and 2b)
- gained an understanding that belonging to a religion can present many challenges (AT1a and 2b)
- been able to express their own views on ways to counter anti-Semitism and Islamaphobia (AT2d and 2e).

Skills involved

Pupils will be:
- thinking about what is essential to practise a religion
- discussing the challenges for some people of belonging to a religion
- using a range of sources to identify the effects of prejudice and discrimination.

Information

This lesson introduces the concept of religious persecution and the challenges of belonging to faith communities. By the very nature of the subject content, some pupils may find this lesson challenges certain attitudes and values. Teachers may choose to amend the materials to suit the particular local issues. The lesson could act as an introduction to the topic or development of previous learning on the Shoah or Genocide. The lesson particularly focuses on the effect of anti-Semitism and Islamaphobia in Britain.

A further area of development would be to focus on religious groups within specific countries, for example:
- Bosnia (Roman Catholics, Serbian Orthodox, Muslims)
- India (Christians, Hindus, Muslims, Sikhs)
- Indonesia (Christians, Muslims)
- Middle East (Christians, Jews and Muslims)
- Sri Lanka (Hindus, Buddhists).

Attacks on religions by governments could also be an area of focus, for example:
- communist oppression of Buddhists and Christians in China
- attacks on Christians and Animists in Sudan.

Use of ICT

Research: To use the Amnesty International website (www.amnesty.org.uk) for more examples of religious discrimination.
Communication: To record findings and present them to others. In Activity 1 pupils could present their circle using ICT and in Activity 3 the list of questions could be presented using ICT. The activity on Worksheet 1.7, which develops Activity 2, asks pupils to write an e-mail.
ICT Resource: See *Framework RE 3 ICT Resource* Teacher's Notes (below).

Activities

Many of the activities focus on AT2 and pupils may have personal experiences which they either want to share or wish not to be reminded of. Pupils should only be asked to share their responses where it is appropriate. Many of the activities ask pupils to reflect on the challenges of belonging to a religious community and to express insights into human relationships.

Activity 1 (AT2b)

Pupils are asked to order a range of different religious practices in terms of how important they think they are.

From pupils' results a class graph could be made. Pupils should be encouraged to look into the implications of each element for the person, the family and the community. For example, who would be effected by the right to have festival days off from school and what would be the implications for school life? It is important that pupils remember that they are considering what a religious person should have a **right** to.

Activity 2 (AT1a, AT1g and AT2b)
Worksheet 1.7

Pupils are asked to compare two sources. The newspaper source supplies more factual detail while the personal account gives a picture of the effect on the individual. Pupils should draw out particular significant details, for example, the event happened on Thursday night before a Friday when many people attend a Mosque, or the significance of the pig's head. The activity should make pupils aware of the role of the media and the press in reporting such incidents.

Worksheet 1.7 builds on this activity to explore different ways of reducing attacks. In groups pupils are asked to discuss four projects using their knowledge of the situations and set criteria. Then they are expected to compose e-mails in which they will be expected to justify the reasons for their choices.

Activity 3(AT2b)

Using a range of stimuli pupils should be made aware of the different types of anti-Semitism and Islamaphobia. The first part of the activity asks pupils to categorise the different examples, although some may be considered in two categories, for example, the graffiti on the grave could be considered as an attack on a person (through trauma) as well as an attack on a place.

In the second part of this activity teachers may direct pupils to the image and story that they think will provide most challenge for pupils. A writing frame with a bank of key words may be a helpful support for some pupils. For pupils requiring further challenge they could write up two accounts for a tabloid and a broadsheet newspaper.

Now try this (extension work) (AT2e and AT2b)

Pupils are expected to apply their understanding from the unit into their response.

A bank of words may be used to support or extend certain pupils, such as faith; commitment; eternal life.

Suggestions for homework and follow-up work

1 Produce a piece of creative work on discrimination in the modern world. This could be a poem, a piece of artwork or a collage of pictures and short pieces of writing.
2 Select one person from the Amnesty International website who has been discriminated against because of their religion. Prepare a short case study to share with the rest of the class.

Framework RE 3 ICT Resource Teacher's Notes

Starter activity

The questions in this activity set the context for the unit and reintroduce relevant terms, for example Islamaphobia, which have been used in previous years.

Answers

1 True

2 True

3 False – Jews were expelled from England in the 1200s

4 True

Main activity

This activity is a good preparation for Activity Three in the Pupil's Book (pages 24–5). Pupils look at each picture in turn and decide who is affected by the attacks and how they are affected. This activity should support visual learners.

There are three pictures in total, one on each screen. Click on the arrow at the bottom of the screen to go on to the next.

Suggested answers

There are no set correct answers – the importance is in the reasoning.

1 Relatives, the public

2 Worshippers, the public

3 Worshippers, local community, other faith communities.

Plenary activity

This activity recaps key concepts from the lesson. Pupils should take it in turns to guess a letter until they can guess the phrases, ideally before the hangman is drawn.

Answers

1 Everyone has the right to freedom of thought, conscience and religion

2 Human Rights

3 Amnesty International

FRAMEWORK RE 3
Worksheet 1.1

1. In Activity One in the pupil book (page 2) you are asked to select captions for pictures 1–6. Work with a partner and decide which you think is the most fitting caption and write in the table below. One example has been done for you.

Picture 1	**Many people wear something special to show they belong to a religion *for example* many Sikh males will wear a turban.**
Picture 2	
Picture 3	
Picture 4	
Picture 5	
Picture 6	

2. Now look through the rest of the Pupil's Book and select three more pictures which show the impact of religion.

Picture 7 **On page:**	
Picture 8 **On page:**	
Picture 9 **On page:**	

FRAMEWORK RE 3

Worksheet 1.2

Use this worksheet to help you with Activity Two. The statements and concepts below can be used to support your answers.

Headscarves ban – girl pupil sent home for wearing the hijab

Pope Says No To Use of Condoms

'I became a churchgoer so my son could go to a Church school'

Prince Charles Visits Local Gurdwara

Church helps local refugee family

New Kosher Restaurant will help Jewish Community

Sikhs worship in a Gurdwara.	The Pope is the leader of the Roman Catholic Church.
'Believing women … should draw their veils over their bosoms and not display their beauty except to their husbands.' (Quran, Surah 24:31)	'From one human being he created all races on Earth and made them live throughout the whole earth.' (Bible, Acts 17:26)
The *Humanae Vitae* declaration of Pope Paul VI stated that sex should always be open to the possibility of creating new life.	Prince Charles is considered the defender of faiths within Britain.
Prince Charles is a member of the Church of England.	It is illegal to wear a hijab, or any other signs of religious commitment, to schools in France.
A Shochet recites a blessing over an animal before it is slaughtered and passed to a kosher butcher.	The book of Leviticus contains the animals that Jews can eat.

FRAMEWORK RE 3

Worksheet 1.3

For each of the following parts of your life, listed in Section A, write down who or what from Section B had or will have a major influence on it.

Section A

What happened at birth

What you believe will happen after you die

What festivals you celebrate

What is important to you

What you don't eat

Which important moral decisions you make

Who you might marry

What you want to happen to you after you die

Section B
- Myself
- Family members
- Family tradition
- Friends

- Conscience
- Religious teachings
- Other

FRAMEWORK RE 3
Worksheet 1.4

Where do you work?

I work in Open House which provides a shelter for homeless children in Brazil. A place where children can wash and get clean clothes and a meal. We also run a programme of games and education.

Why didn't you choose to help people in England?

I have helped people in England but think there are greater needs in other parts of the world. When I saw so many children living on the streets in Brazil I decided to stay and try to make a difference.

Were you ever afraid?

I often get afraid when the street children fight each other. They can change personality very quickly, and become extremely violent and dangerous.

How is your work making a difference?

In Open House children are educated socially and spiritually, as well as academically. They learn how to wash themselves, to eat, and to sleep at a normal time of day. They learn how to solve disputes without violence. Most importantly they learn how to value themselves and others around them.

Where is God in all this?

I believe that God is in the centre of everything we do. I believe it was God who called me and I had the faith to follow.

FRAMEWORK RE 3

Worksheet 1.5

To complete this worksheet you will need to get information from two different sources. You will need to use the information from the interview with Matthew (see Worksheet 1.4) and from one of the following websites:

- www.streetchildren.org.uk
- www.mnmmr.org.br
- www.whiteband.org
- www.makepovertyhistory.org
- www.mkarcher.com.

Why do so many children become street children?

What dangers do they face on the street?

What dangers do people who work on the street face?

FRAMEWORK RE 3

Worksheet 1.6

Use this worksheet to help you with your homework.

Different denominations of Judaism

Ashkenazi – Jews who settled in Europe and commonly spoke Yiddish.

Sephardic – Jews who have originally come from Spain, Portugal or the Orient. They often use Ladino as a common language.

Orthodox – Traditional Judaism. Usually Jews who do not agree with changing practices.

Progressive – Non-Orthodox denominations, sometimes called Reform Jews.

Liberal – Found the Reform movement too restrictive. Maintain that keeping the commandments is optional. Regard everyone brought up as a Jew to be Jewish.

Falasha Jew – Ethiopian Jews who claim descent from King Solomon. Many went to live in Israel in the 1980s.

Secular Jew – Jews who do not normally consider religion as important and keep little or nothing of the traditions.

Zionist – Belief that the land of Israel is the homeland of Jewish people. Zionists do not have to be Jews and Jews don't have to be Zionists.

Task
Using the statements as evidence how would you describe Nathan, Beckie and Leah?

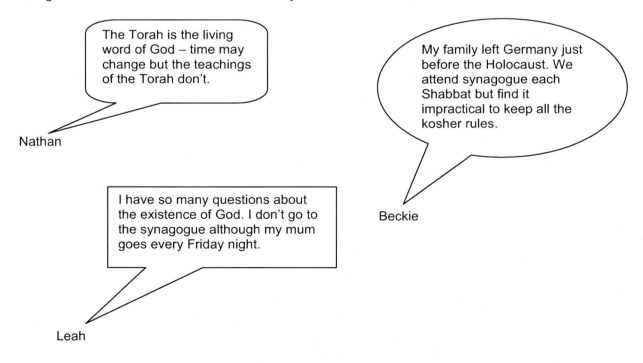

The Torah is the living word of God – time may change but the teachings of the Torah don't.

Nathan

My family left Germany just before the Holocaust. We attend synagogue each Shabbat but find it impractical to keep all the kosher rules.

Beckie

I have so many questions about the existence of God. I don't go to the synagogue although my mum goes every Friday night.

Leah

FRAMEWORK RE 3

Worksheet 1.7

Use this worksheet to help you with Activity Two. It runs over two pages.

Situation

The local community is concerned about a recent rise of anti-Semitic and Islamaphobic attacks which seem to be carried out by groups of people between the ages of 14–18. So far no one has been hurt but local faith members are worried about the rise in graffiti, name-calling and broken windows. In the area there are three local secondary schools: One for Roman Catholic pupils; one for Muslim pupils; and one for pupils of all or no faiths – although few Roman Catholic or Muslim pupils attend this school.

The council has given you £5000 to try and stop these attacks and four proposals have been submitted. They expect you to make your decision of which proposal to adopt meeting two criteria:

Which project will have a long-term effect?

Which project will benefit the greatest number of people?

Task

Get into groups of four.

- Put the four project cards face down in the middle of the table.

- Each member of the group takes it in turn to read one of the project cards and gives a reason why they think it should be supported.

- Look at the criteria again and put the cards in rank order for which you think would be most effective.

- Write an e-mail to justify your selection.

FRAMEWORK RE 3
Worksheet 1.7 (continued)

Project 1

The funding would be used for extra security at the main places of worship and the cemetery. CCTV would be installed and a security guard would work one evening a week.

Project 2

All three schools would have more lessons on Islam and Judaism so that all pupils would be aware of the religions.

Project 3

The funding would be used to run a youth club one night a week for three years. This would allow teenagers of all faiths and none to mix together. The youth club would be held at different places of worship.

Project 4

The funding would be used to print leaflets and advertise in local papers to explain what is happening and why it is wrong.

UNIT 2: WHAT IS THE IMPACT OF DIFFERENT RELIGIONS ON THE COMMUNITY?

INTRODUCTION

The purpose of this unit is to allow pupils to relate the fact of people being religious to the concept of community. Throughout the unit pupils are given opportunities to develop and consolidate their knowledge and understanding of world religions.

The unit therefore develops pupils' skills of interpreting and applying their learning to life today, and so covers some of the required themes of the Framework.

Contents

The first lesson of this unit begins by looking at the importance of community and the relationship between local community and faith communities. Lessons 2 and 3 consider the reasons that many faiths take an active role in supporting local communities and the some of the ways that they do this.

The fourth and fifth lessons allow pupils to express their own views on two contemporary issues concerning the role of faith communities: The fourth lesson looks at the role of faith schools and the fifth (and final) lesson of the unit considers why some religious communities choose to live together.

Appendices

- Appendix A: Record of achievement chart.
- Appendix B: Grid identifying the various learning styles, skills and methods employed in each lesson.

APPENDIX A

FRAMEWORK RE 3: RECORD OF ACHIEVEMENT
UNIT 2

PUPIL NAME: _____ GROUP: _____ TEACHER: _____

LESSON	AT1 Activity	AT1 Mark	AT2 Activity	AT2 Mark
1			1	
	2		2	
	3			
	NTT		NTT	
2			1	
			2	
	3			
			NTT	
3	1			
			2	
	3		3	
4	NTT			
	1			
	2		2	
			3	
5			NTT	
	1		1	
	2		2	
	3		3	
	NTT		NTT	
LEVEL				

NOTES ON PROGRESS:

TARGETS:

Signed (Pupil) _____ Signed (Teacher) _____

APPENDIX B

UNIT 2: COVERAGE OF LEARNING ACTIVITIES, STYLES, METHODS, SKILLS

	Lesson 1	Lesson 2	Lesson 3	Lesson 4	Lesson 5
Most likely					
Classification	✖	✖		✖	✖
Odd one out					
Reveal			✖		
Sequencing					
Show me					
Reflective questioning	✖	✖	✖	✖	✖
Multiple choice					
Ranking					
Drag and drop				✖	
Matching	✖				✖
Filling in gaps				✖	
Writing	✖	✖	✖	✖	✖
Brainstorming	✖	✖	✖	✖	✖
Discussion	✖	✖	✖	✖	✖
Comparing	✖			✖	
Investigating		✖		✖	
Questioning	✖	✖	✖	✖	✖
Explaining	✖	✖	✖	✖	✖
Giving accounts	✖				
Mind map		✖	✖		
Evaluating		✖	✖		✖
Imagining		✖		✖	
Analysing	✖		✖		✖
Synthesising				✖	
Empathising	✖		✖	✖	
Criticising					
Negotiating	✖	✖	✖	✖	✖
Deciding	✖	✖	✖	✖	✖
Expressing clearly	✖	✖	✖	✖	✖
Listening	✖	✖	✖	✖	✖
Interpreting	✖	✖		✖	
Applying	✖	✖			✖
Responding	✖	✖	✖	✖	✖
Observing	✖	✖	✖		
Learning styles					
Kinaesthetic					
Auditory		✖			
Visual	✖	✖			

1. WHY ARE COMMUNITIES IMPORTANT?

Pupil's Book pages 28–31

Aim
The aim of this lesson is to teach pupils the role of the various communities within an area and the connection between belonging to a range of different communities.

Learning objectives
By the end of this unit pupils should have:
- expressed insights into their own and others' views on the importance of belonging (AT2d and 2e)
- gained a knowledge and understanding of the importance of belonging to a faith community for many people (AT1c and 1g)
- defined and applied the concept of community (AT1h).

Skills involved
Pupils will be:
- defining and applying the concept of community
- recognising the importance of belonging to a faith community for many people
- expressing insights into their own and others' views on the importance of belonging.

Information
In the first part of the lesson pupils are expected to explore the meaning of their local community for themselves and others. Further details of The Community Spirit Project referred to can be found in *Altaring Liverpool* by Liverpool Community Spirit (ISBN: 1905089007).

The second part of the lesson expects pupils to interrogate a range of quotes to analyse the role of a religious community within the local community (or vice versa). This dual sense of belonging will be referred to in Unit 5, Lesson 6, where the conflict is explored between religious and state demands and expectations.

Use of ICT
Research: To use the Internet to identify the places of worship within the local area. Your local council website should list these.
Communication: In Activity 2 pupils could create their concept map using ICT. The 'Now try this' activity may give pupils the opportunity to create a logo using an ICT package.
ICT Resource: See *Framework RE 3 ICT Resource Teacher's Notes*, page 33.

Activity 1 (AT2e) <u>Worksheet 2.1</u>
This activity allows pupils to consider the different attributes of the communities they belong to and their different responsibilities within them. The first part of the activity should help pupils to draw up the criteria of what constitutes a community. They are then expected to identify the features of the many communities they belong to.

Worksheet 2.1 supports pupils in identifying the different features of the communities they belong to. Some pupils will readily identify the external features of the communities – for example, what people wear, when they hold events – but may need support to identify intrinsic features, such as the aim of the community and whether it is a permanent feature.

Activity 2 (AT1c and AT2d)
In this activity pupils identify the wide range of different benefits that members may get out of different places within their community. This activity should overtly contribute to spiritual development, which could be supported by the homework/extension task.

There is no definitive list of key concepts but they may include memory/pride/sense of God/spirit/working for the same goal.

There are many different ways of creating a concept or mind map and by Year 9, pupils will often be able to adapt a particular style to suit the purpose or content. If pupils are new to creating a concept map then for this occasion they should write **A special place** in the middle of their page and from this draw out four branches in different colours with each of the reasons placed at the end of the branch.

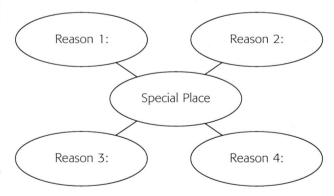

Activity 3 (AT1g)
In this activity pupils are required to match quotes with the benefits of belonging to a faith community. During the activity pupils should begin to understand the wide range of activities that take place within faith communities. They could also be made aware of the fact that many people have to travel outside their local community in order to join their faith community.

Possible answers may be:

1 Vijay; Parminder; Leon; Nasima.
2 Leah; Fran.
3 Adel; Nasima; Leah.
4 Vijay; Adel; Parminder; Leon; Nasima; Fran.
5 Vijay; Adel; Parminder; Rebekah; Fran.
6 Vijay; Adel; Leon.
7 Vijay.

Now try this (extension work) (AT1h and AT2e)

This requires pupils to use linguistic or visual skills by creating a teaching resource which allows them to show their own understanding of the term 'community'. The resource would need to describe a sense of bonding or shared purpose, for example, drawing a crowd of people would not express community.

Suggestions for homework and follow-up work

1 Discuss why you think an altar was used in the Liverpool Project and what other symbols you think would be appropriate.
2 Ask ten people in your community where they would place their altar (or alternative symbol) and why. Bring your results into class to create a wall display. Make a list of key concepts to put on the display showing why these places are so special.

Framework RE 3 ICT Resource Teacher's Notes

Starter activity

This activity works well for independent learning, or as a paired or group activity. By selecting appropriate questions pupils should show that they understand the concept of community. There are no set correct answers. It may be appropriate to give some pupils a resource bank of questions in order to identify which would be best to gain their answer, for example:

● Do you all live in the same area?

● Do you all attend the same club?

● What are your favourite foods?

● Do you believe in God?

● How often do you meet together?

Main activity

In this activity pupils have to correct the spellings of the different religions and then identify which quote is linked to which religion. Even at GCSE level many candidates lose marks for the incorrect spelling of religious traditions.

Within each quote there are clues to identify the religion which test pupils' knowledge of key terms.

Answers

1 Kristianity – Christianity – d) I am following an Alpha course within the church.

2 Hindooism – Hinduism – a) I am going to the mandir to celebrate Divali.

3 Jewdaism – Judaism – e) My grandfather went to the same synagogue as I go to.

4 Izlams – Islam – b) At the mosque we support Islamic Relief and learn Arabic.

5 Seekhism –Sikhism – c) I feel part of the community at the gurdwara.

Plenary activity

In this activity pupils are asked to reflect upon the attributes of their own communities. This is done by asking them to associate a series of words and pictures with communities they belong to. Each combination of word and picture is on a separate screen. There are eight in total. Click on the arrow at the bottom of the screen to move on to the next. Prior to the activity teachers need to provide a safe and secure classroom environment by telling the pupils they will not need to share their reflections unless they want to.

It may be that some pupils are unable to think of a place for each word and picture. A further development of this activity would be to see how many pupils are unable to associate particular words with their communities and draw a graph or pie chart to represent this.

2. WHY DO PEOPLE HELP OTHERS IN THE COMMUNITY?

Pupil's Book pages 32–35

Aim

The aim of this lesson is to teach pupils why many religious and non-religious people consider it important to serve others in the community.

Learning objectives

By the end of the lesson pupils should have:

- thought about what we mean by service (AT2a and 2d)
- understood that different religious people have similar and different attitudes to service (AT1a)
- gained an understanding of religious and non-religious beliefs about service (AT1d)
- been able to express their own ideas about service (AT2c).

Skills involved

Pupils will be:

- identifying why people decide to serve others in the community
- investigating a range of religious and non-religious views on service
- expressing their own views concerning what is meant by service.

Information

In this lesson the focus is on the reasons why people consider that service is important. As a lead into a GCSE course, the lesson could be developed to focus on a biographical account of how someone has served a community in their life and investigating why they do so (see the work of Mathew Archer on pages 16–17 of the Pupil's Book).

Use of ICT

Research: To use the Internet to find further information on the beliefs contained in this lesson, or on the attitudes of religious people towards service.

Communication: Pupils could produce the worksheet concept map electronically.

ICT Resource: See *Framework RE 3 ICT Resource Teacher's Notes*, page 35.

Activity 1 (AT2d)

This activity is expected to provoke discussion by focusing upon the sequence of pictures. It is expected that pupils will understand the importance of helping each other and that working on your own would not have got the people out of the hole. Pupils may also consider the types of

people who might need most help. References could be made to recent disasters where people have supported each other and worked together. The order of pictures should be 2, 4, 3, 5, 1.

In the second part of the activity, expect pupils to offer a range of different titles. Some pupils will relate to what they actually see, for example, 'Trapped', while other pupils will reflect their conceptual understanding, for example, 'The Ultimate Society', 'God's Dream', 'Do to your neighbour as you would have done to you' etc.

Activity 2 (AT2a and AT2d)

In this activity pupils are expected to be able to distinguish between caring and service using a continuum line. In the second part of the activity, some pupils might find it useful to draw their examples, for example, 'I show I care when I buy my ill neighbour some flowers', 'I show I respect someone when I stand as they enter the room'. Pupils should be encouraged to recognise that to serve requires some form of sacrifice. To help this, references could be made to people within their own community, for example, the mayor, or to other parts of the book, such as Unit 1 Lesson 4.

Activity 3 (AT1a and AT1d) Worksheet 2.2

After reading through the variety of teachings and sacred texts pupils should be able to formulate the table. Although there will be some similar responses between the religions it is important that pupils recognise key concepts such as love in action; sense of unity; compassion; responsibility; a command; form of worship.

When pupils are completing the second part of the activity they should be able to use appropriately the concept of vocation. They may refer to how Matthew gives financially and of his time; how he cares for people from outside his own community; and the different ways that he serves the street children.

On Worksheet 2.2 pupils underline the types of people that the teachings refer to and the reasons why people should serve. They then summarise their findings by creating a concept map.

Now try this (extension work) (AT2c)

This extension activity requires pupils to analyse and to suggest situations. For some pupils requiring further challenge they may wish to identify examples locally and globally.

Suggestions for homework and follow-up work

1 Investigate the lives of different people who have served the local or global community, focus particularly on the rationale of why they chose to do this.

2 Reflect what is meant by 'talisman' and consider your own talisman.

3 Consider if you need to be religious to serve other people.

Framework RE 3 ICT Resource Teacher's Notes

Starter activity

In this activity pupils should negotiate in groups the order they think the pictures should be in and drag and drop them into place (this supports Activity One in the Pupil's Book, pages 32–3). When pupils are considering the captions on the following screens they should focus on the message of each individual picture. As this is a group activity pupils should be aware of the need to negotiate their answers. Click on the arrow at the bottom of the screen to move on to the next.

Answers

1 Picture 2

2 Picture 4

3 Picture 3

4 Picture 5

5 Picture 1

Main activity

Through this activity pupils investigate pictures that show different aspects of service towards others. These pictures also appear in the Pupil's Book. This activity will help develop pupils' investigation skills as they ascertain how religious teachings support the charitable actions shown in each picture.

There are no correct answers but pupils should be able to justify their decisions.

There are four pictures in total, one on each screen. Click on the arrow at the bottom of the screen to move on to the next.

Plenary activity

Pupils should work either individually or in small groups to decide the main learning points from the lesson. Each group should then provide a summary point to complete the boxes.

Suggested answers

The main points might include reference to the following:

● Service is often considered as love in action and usually requires personal sacrifice.

● All religions consider it important to show active service to others.

● Buddhism and the importance of compassion for all beings.

● For Christians, Jesus was a role model of service when he washed the disciples' feet.

● Humanists believe it is important to treat others as you would want to be treated.

● For Sikhs, seva can be through any work done without gain.

3. WHAT ROLES DO RELIGIONS PLAY IN THE COMMUNITY?

Pupil's Book pages 36–39

Aim
The aim of this lesson is to raise the awareness of the range of activities faith communities support.

Learning objectives
By the end of this unit pupils should have:
- interpreted a traditional Jewish story (AT1g)
- gained a knowledge and understanding of different ways faith groups support communities (AT1a)
- recognised the role of Faithworks in local communities (AT1a)
- made links and expressed insights between religious teachings and faith in action (AT1a, 1e and 2c).

Skills involved
Pupils will be:
- interpreting a story
- using a range of sources to investigate the role religions can play within a community
- expressing an opinion concerning their local community.

Information
Many local authorities are now working with faith groups when considering the regeneration of local areas. In many inner city areas there are faith councils who represent the voice of the faiths within the area.

Through the range of pictures in Activity 3, pupils explore how different faith groups put the teachings of service to the community in action. The introduction of Faithworks shows how some religious organisations also try to challenge people's attitudes. Since its launch in 2003, Faithworks has been working to inspire Christians to take an active role in the community. One particular project is the work they do to challenge people's attitudes to the traveller and gypsy community. Introducing pupils to the case study of Johnny Delaney will help to counter stereotypes and could lead to further work concerning prejudice and discrimination against the travelling community, in addition to an investigation of the traditions and cultures of Romany and traveller communities.

The National Framework emphasises the need to challenge stereotypes that can lead to discrimination. Trevor Phillips, Chairman for Racial Equality said 'gypsies and travellers probably suffer the most discrimination in the country'. Faithworks suggest a number of ways that Christians can support travellers, such as:
- praying for them
- learning more about traveller lifestyles to stop uninformed comments and prejudice
- writing a letter to local council's to request proper sites for travellers
- writing to newspapers if they make prejudiced or stereotypical comments about travellers.

Use of ICT
Research: To find out details of the action of local faith groups; to further research the action and role of Faithworks.
Communication: Activity 2 could be presented using ICT.
ICT Resource: See *Framework RE 3 ICT Resource* Teacher's Notes, page 37.

Activity 1 (AT1g)
This activity requires pupils to interpret and summarise a traditional Jewish story. In their text messages pupils should recognise that there are many different ways and talents that can support the community. The activity may lead onto exploring the importance of community volunteers and active citizenship. There is no right or wrong title but the range of titles allows pupils to consider if the identification of the tradition is more important than the actual message.

Activity 2 (AT2e)
In this activity pupils are asked to give a balance of justified viewpoints. This is an important skill to develop in order to answer evaluation questions in GCSE examinations. For some pupils it may be helpful to provide a bank of statements for them to select which they consider the most valid arguments. Pupils should be aware that they do not have to agree with the statement but they have to show they can express another point of view and can use evidence to justify their point of view.
For the first statement arguments could include:
- It is up to the council and government to take action not faith groups.
- Many people don't believe in a religion and might be opposed to faith groups taking a role.
- There should be a separation between religion and social issues.
- Faith groups might take on such a role to try to get people to become members of that faith.

For the second statement arguments could include:
- All faiths consider it important to serve the community.

- To be a faith member means that you must care for others and put in action the teachings of religion.
- Many faith communities have to challenge social injustices.

Activity 3 (AT1a and AT2c) ⟨Worksheet 2.3⟩

In the first part of this activity pupils investigate a range of visual sources and make links with previous learning. Pupils could complete the activity from recall and then be given an opportunity to refer to the previous lesson to add any further relevant details. In the first part of the activity pupils should be encouraged to use a range of religious terms in their answers.

Worksheet 2.3 extends this activity to direct pupils to identify specific projects within their community, for example, collecting clothes in Islamic Relief clothes banks or activities within local places of worship such as the local church holding activities for senior citizens. Pupils could use a variety of sources to complete the worksheet.

The final part of the activity allows pupils to recap on the work they have covered so far in this chapter by completing an acrostic. Pupils should be challenged to use a wide a range of religious terminology. A further challenge could be created by pupils answering from just one religious tradition.

Key words may include:

Seva (Sikh reference); stereotypes; shelter; sacrifice; sweetness (Buddhist reference); sharing; Sheep and Goats parable (Christian reference); strangers; selfless work (Hindu reference)

Everyone; empathy; eternity

Religions; respecting; responsible (Jewish reference); religious worship; rewards

Vocation; value;

Inclusion; increase happiness (Humanist reference)

Challenge; company; community; caring; charity

Everyone; empathy; eternity

Now try this (extension work) (AT1e)

The interpretation of the quote should include some reference to the role of the individual. Pupils may consider how this quote applies to times of great disasters and suffering.

Suggestions for homework and follow-up work

1 Draw the outline of a local place of worship and inside write the activities that are held for the different sectors of the community. A helpful start would be to look closely at the evidence of the notice board in the place of worship.
2 Devise a logo for Faithworks which reflects the community focus of their work.

Framework RE 3 ICT Resource Teacher's Notes

Starter activity

Pupils take it in turns to remove a piece of the jigsaw and then guess what the picture is. The picture shows a Buddhist monk in Cambodia supporting a patient who has lost a limb due to the landmines in the area. It also appears on page 39 of the Pupil's Book. Once pupils have guessed the picture they could then discuss the motivation for the Buddhist monk's attitudes. This may draw on their previous learning, for example the importance of the Five Precepts. Pupils should then suggest a title or caption to the picture which is different to that in the Pupil's Book.

Main activity

This activity supports Activity Three in the Pupil's Book (page 39). It gives pupils the opportunity to study the pictures and to investigate them for clues before coming to a conclusion about which religious tradition the person giving help belongs to. The correct religion should be written in the text box. Pupils should also try to develop a caption to say which teaching from the religion they have identified would motivate the person to act in this way.

There are four pictures in total, one on each screen. Click on the arrow at the bottom of the screen to go on to the next.

Answers

1 Hinduism

2 Christianity

3 Buddhism

4 Sikhism

Plenary activity

Before beginning this activity it is important to establish a calm classroom atmosphere, for example by changing pupils' seating arrangements and lighting. Clear guidelines should be given concerning behavioural expectations during the exercise. Appropriate music could be played as pupils read the poem.

Pupils should be given the opportunity to reflect upon the key question before seeing the poem and the picture of Johnny Delaney (on a separate screen accessed by clicking on 'start'). You may want to recap on who Johnny was and what happened to him before the poem begins (see Pupil's Book, page 37). Encourage pupils to write their responses on soluble paper, which can be placed in water after the lesson.

The purpose of the activity is to encourage pupils to reflect using their own views – they may make specific reference to inequalities in their own neighbourhoods.

4. WHY ARE THERE DIFFERENT TYPES OF SCHOOLS?

Pupil's Book pages 40–44

Aim
The aim of this lesson is to raise pupils' awareness of the nature of faith schools and to explore their impact upon the individual and wider community.

Learning objectives
By the end of the lesson pupils should have:
- gained an understanding of some of the differences between faith and non-faith schools (AT1a, 1b and 2b)
- been able to express their own views concerning the role of faith schools (AT2b, 2c and 2d)
- selected and prioritised key arguments for and against the existence of faith schools (AT2c and 2e).

Skills involved
Pupils will be:
- identifying different types of faith schools
- considering the differences between faith and non-faith schools
- selecting reasons for and against faith schools.

Use of ICT
Research: For Activity 1 pupils can explore the websites of a range of different local schools and look for evidence of the faith or non-faith nature of the school.

Communication: Pupils can present their evaluation in the worksheet activity using ICT. In the 'Now try this' activity pupils can use ICT to produce a promotional leaflet.

ICT Resource: See *Framework RE 3 ICT Resource Teacher's Notes*, page 39.

Activity 1 (AT1a and AT1b)
This activity supports previous learning by asking pupils to identify relevant evidence to support the identification of different faith traditions. This activity should also make pupils aware of the number of different faith traditions which have their own schools. Expected answers would be as below:

Picture	Religion	Evidence
1	Christian	Nun; stained glass windows; chapel
2	Muslim or Islamic	Islamic symbols; Qur'an and crescent
3	Jewish	Hebrew writing and Hanukiah candles
4	Hindu	Hindu writing; ohm symbol; rangoli patterns

Activity 2 (AT1a and AT2b)

Expected answers to the first part of the activity:

Picture 1 – Shirin (clue: Lord's Prayer), Sophie (clue: retreat)

Picture 2 – Uzma (clue: halal food), Nasima (clue: hijab)

Picture 3 – Anna (clue: Rosh Hashanah)

Picture 4 – Henna (clue: Hinduism)

Bryn, Fran and Salli could attend any school.

In the second part of the activity pupils compare their own school experiences to those that might be present in faith schools. Pupils should realise that many of the elements would be the same, for example, homework, timetables, etc.

Activity 3 (AT2b, AT2c and AT2d)
Worksheet 2.4

In groups pupils are expected to interpret a range of statements and to consider whether they are in support or not of faith schools or are neutral statements. A vital part of this activity is pupils working together and discussing and sharing their own views. These skills will play a substantial role in completing the worksheet evaluation. Worksheet 2.4 is modeled upon the skills required for evaluation questions at GCSE. The activities in this lesson will have built up step-by-step support for completing the task.

Now try this (extension work) (AT2e)

This extension task requires pupils to have understood some of the challenges concerning segregation of schools and to suggest strategies to support people from different faith groups to work together. Some pupils may be able to structure their planning into different categories, for example, activities; food; clothes; worship; etc.

Suggestions for homework and follow-up work

1 A class debate could be arranged from Activity 3.
2 Find out the different types of schools in your local area.

Framework RE 3 ICT Resource Teacher's Notes

Starter activity

The pupils should work in pairs or groups to decide which picture is the odd one out and why. The intended outcome is an extended discussion on the nature of a faith school and the fact that some people are excluded from some schools on the grounds of religion or sex. This could lead to further discussion on whether pupils support the idea of schools being an integrated community.

Answer

The school is the odd one out as, although it is in the community, it is the only place that can select which members of the community can attend.

Main activity

Pupils are required to indicate their strength of feeling about each statement. Although there are no right or wrong answers, they should be able to justify their decisions.

This activity can take place before Activity Two in the Pupil's Book (page 42) and again at the end of the lesson to ascertain whether there have been any changes in views.

There are two statements in total, one on each screen. Click on the arrow at the bottom of the screen to go on to the next.

Plenary activity

Through this activity pupils will be expected to analyse and put in order arguments to support two different statements about faith schools. Arguments can be dragged and dropped alongside the opinion line. There is no set correct order. Once this has been completed pupils can use these arguments as a framework to write an evaluation answer for and against faith schools.

There are two statements in total, one on each screen. Click on the arrow at the bottom of the screen to go on to the next.

5. WHY DO SOME RELIGIOUS COMMUNITIES LIVE APART?

Pupil's Book pages 44–47

Aim

The aim of this lesson is to teach pupils that some religious communities believe it is important to live together as a worshipping community.

Learning objectives

By the end of the lesson pupils should have:

- understood why some religious communities consider it important to live a life with little connection with the wider community (AT1c)
- been able to evaluate the challenges of living a life within a closed community (AT1g, 2b and 2e)
- gained a basic knowledge of the beliefs, practices and values of the Amish (AT1a).

Skills involved

Pupils will be:

- considering why some religious communities live together
- sorting and categorising information from a range of sources
- thinking about the challenges of belonging to religious communities.

Information

The information concerning monasteries will be a recap on previous learning. The emphasis should be on *why* monks and nuns choose to live in a closed environment and the importance of the three rules for the following of their religion.

Since the film *The Witness* there has been an increased interest in the beliefs and practices of the Amish. The Amish are a group of strict Mennonites who settled mainly in the eastern USA at the end of the seventeenth century under the leadership of Jacob Ammann who insisted on strict discipline. They separate themselves from the society around them by keeping the customs and dress of that early time. They do not seek to convert people to become Amish but insist that marriage should always be within practicing members of the religion. The growth of the religion is due to the large size families and there are now about 130,000 members.

Some pupils, through their investigations, will recognise the tensions between interest in this community and public intrusion.

Use of ICT

Research: In the worksheet and homework activity pupils could use the Internet to research more information on the Amish.

Communication: Pupils can present their homework pamphlet using ICT.

ICT Resource: See *Framework RE 3 ICT Resource Teacher's Notes*, on page 41.

Activity 1 (AT1c and AT2b)

In the first part of the activity pupils will reflect upon the implications of the three vows for their own lives. Some pupils will find it easier to access this activity by first writing a diary account for the previous day and then highlighting where a vow of poverty, chastity or obedience would have made an impact.

In the second part of the activity pupils are asked which of the three rules they would find hardest to keep. They should consider short and long term implications.

They could come to their decision by doing a brainstorming exercise, which would explore the considerations. Answers may include:

Poverty	What would happen to the possessions they had?
	What about the possessions that had been 'passed down' to them?
	What would happen if they left the monastery?
	Certain possessions people need.
Chastity	What would happen as they got older and had no family?
	It would be difficult to share their feelings with other people in the monastery.
Obedience	What if they were told to do something they thought was wrong?
	How could they think for themselves?

The third part of the activity provides a range of answers to the question 'Do you think it is a good idea that people live in monasteries and convents?' Pupils have to choose which of the answers support living in a monastery and convent (answers a, c and d) and which answers are against it (answers b and e).

Activity 2 (AT1a and AT2e) Worksheet 2.5

Through this activity pupils are introduced to the Amish community and are asked to complete a table about their beliefs and practices using the evidence provided. They could add to this by carrying out their own research on the Internet about the beliefs and practices of the Amish.

Some students might need support in distinguishing the difference between a *belief* and a *practice*. To support this understanding pupils may be split into two different groups (one 'belief' and one 'practice') and asked to decide on a working definition of 'their' term:

- Belief (something you think is true).
- Practice (doing something rather than thinking about it).

Each group could then be given five minutes to look through their textbook and to identify examples of the term. Unit 2, Lessons 3 and 4 will give many examples. The results can then be fed back to the whole class.

Worksheet 2.5 allows pupils to reflect upon the information they have read and provides a good opportunity for self-assessment.

Examples may include:

Beliefs

- They don't believe in war.
- People shouldn't go against the Ten Commandments.
- It is important to live separately so that they are not polluted.
- It is the people, not the building, that is the Church.

Practices

- The men don't grow moustaches.
- At weddings the bride wears blue or purple.
- They don't usually allow photos of their faces.
- The don't own phones or TVs.
- They don't use electricity.

Activity 3 (AT1g)

In this activity pupils should reflect upon the aspects of contemporary society which would be considered as a pollutant (something which makes something impure or spoils it). To support some pupils, a range of newspapers and magazines could be explored to identify possibilities, for example drugs, alcohol, lottery, etc.

Now try this (extension work) (AT2e)

In this activity pupils are introduced to the conflict between religious beliefs and commercialisation. Pupils may consider a range of views including:

- If people don't witness it for themselves then they won't understand.
- It makes a religious community appear 'odd'.

Suggestions for homework and follow-up work

1 Use ICT to produce a pamphlet which would explain the Amish lifestyle to tourists.

2 Identify other examples of how tourism promotes or intrudes upon aspects of religious life. You could relate your answer to examples from your own travels, such as tourist visits to places of worship.

Framework RE 3 ICT Resource Teacher's Notes

Starter activity

Pupils could be asked to consider the statements and decide for themselves which order they most agree with, and be ready to justify their decisions. A class consensus could then be taken and put onto the screen. This feeds into Activities One and Two (Pupil's Book pages 45 and 46) as it introduces pupils to many of the distinctive characteristics of the Amish.

Main activity

In this activity six pictures from Pupil's Book pages 46–47 are used, each on a separate screen. Pupils should be allowed to examine each picture individually for a minute in order to think of a question that would help them to find out more about the Amish way of life. The question can be written in the box by the appropriate number and could form the basis of a research task. Click on the arrow at the bottom of the screen to go on to the next picture.

This activity will support visual learners and also discussion skills as pupils identify the distinctive features of the Amish.

Plenary activity

Pupils choose key features of their life to write in one side of the Venn diagram and key features of the life of the Amish to write in the other side. They should try to think of at least three similarities to write in the middle. Using the Venn diagram, a discussion can take place comparing Amish life to pupils' lives. Through this activity pupils are learning about the Amish and reflecting upon the similarities and differences in their own life-stances.

This activity will lead pupils into an expression of their own and Amish views on questions of identity and belonging and a consideration of the challenges of belonging to a religion in the contemporary world. Responses such as these would be indicative of level six.

FRAMEWORK RE 3
Worksheet 2.1

Use this worksheet to help you with Activity One.

Tasks

1   Consider two communities you belong to which are not religious communities. In the A and B circles write the name of each and any distinctive features they have. There are some ideas at the bottom of the worksheet. In the shared circle write down any similarities of the two communities.

2   Now consider a religious community and its characteristics. Which characteristics are the same as the school and hobby communities and which are different?

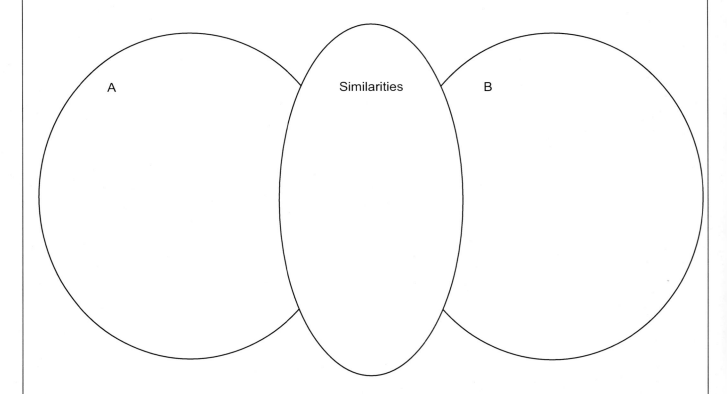

Ideas

- Do you celebrate any special times together?
- Do you wear distinctive clothing?
- Do you meet together at a special place?
- Do you have a shared vision and beliefs?
- Can anyone join?

- Do you have to do something to show you are a member of that community?
- Do you have a ceremony when you join that community?
- Is it for one age group?
- Is there a leader?
- What type of authority does the leader have?

FRAMEWORK RE 3

Worksheet 2.2

Use this worksheet to help you with Activity Three.

Tasks

Underline the types of people that should be served according to the different teachings.

In a different colour underline the reasons why people should serve.

Create a concept map to illustrate your findings.

Hinduism

Service of others is love in action. It shows unselfishness and the sense of unity between people. Every selfless act comes from God because it shows no sense of the separate doer.

'Strive constantly to serve the welfare of the world; by devotion to selfless work one attains the supreme goal of life.'
Bhagavad Gita Chapter 4

Buddhism

Buddhism teaches that people should have compassion for all beings. According to the Dhammapada, serving those in need is not a burden but a sweetness. It is an opportunity to share happiness and do something good before leaving this life.

'To have friends in need is sweet
And to share happiness,
And to have done something good
Before leaving this life is sweet.'
Dhammapada 23

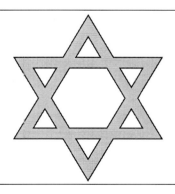

Judaism

Judaism teaches that everyone is responsible for each other. Those who do not perform kind acts do not know God.

'All men are responsible for one another.
Even a poor man who himself subsists on charity should give charity.
He who prays for his fellowman,
While he himself has the same need,
Will be answered first.'
Sanhedrin 27a

FRAMEWORK RE 3

Worksheet 2.2 (continued)

Christianity
Christian scriptures teach that giving is better than receiving. This is seen by the words and actions of Jesus. In the Gospel of John, Jesus washes his disciples feet, giving a practical example of humble service. In the parable of the Sheep and Goats, Jesus taught that those who serve others are praised and those who do not are condemned. The letters in the New Testament also show how important it is for Christians to serve others.

'Do not forget to entertain strangers, for by so doing some people have entertained angels without knowing it.'
Hebrews 13:2

'So whether you eat or drink or whatever you do, do it all for the glory of God.'
1 Corinthians 10:31

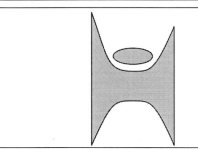

Humanism
Humanists believe that communities can work well and increase happiness by people caring for young and old and treating others in a way you want to be treated.

'Treat other people as you'd want to be treated in their situation; don't do things you wouldn't want to have done to you.'
British Humanist Association 1999

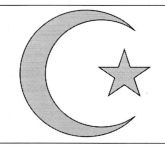

Islam
The Qur'an and Hadith teach that Muslims should help everyone. Being a true Muslim means that you have must serve others and seek no reward for yourself.

'They feed with food the needy wretch, the orphan, and the prisoners, for love of Him, saying "We wish for no reward nor thanks from you".'
Qur'an 76 8–9

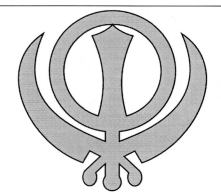

Sikhism
Service is very important in Sikhism and is a means of serving, honouring or worshipping. God is not separate from people and so service to humanity is a form of worship. True service (seva) can be through menial or creative work but must be without gain and in humility.

'Cursed are the hands and feet that engage not in seva.'
Bhai Gurdas 27.10

'A place in God's court can only be attained if we do service to others in the world.'
Guru Granth Sahib 26

FRAMEWORK RE 3

Worksheet 2.3

Use this worksheet to help you with Activity Three.

Task
Choose a religion and research how it supports your local community. Then label the signpost with your chosen religion and fill in the answers to the questions under the direction signs.

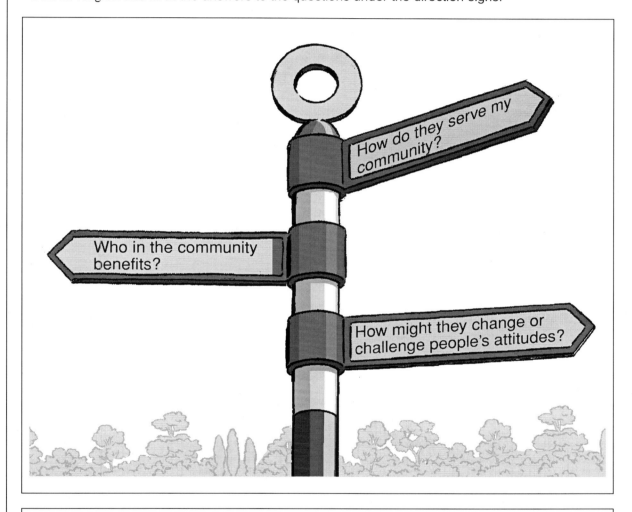

I gained my evidence by:

Using the Internet

Visiting a place of worship

Collecting information from newspapers

Interviewing people

Any other ways _____

FRAMEWORK RE 3

Worksheet 2.4

Use this worksheet to help you with Activity Three.

> **There should be no faith based schools in Britain. Do you agree? Give reasons to support your view showing you have considered other views.**

The evaluation template should help you complete this piece of work. Remember to include the main arguments you have selected from Activity Three and to make sure that you explain them in your own words. There is a word bank at the bottom of the page to support your arguments.

My view about faith based schools is _____
_____
_____

This is mainly because _____
_____
_____
_____

Another argument which supports this view is _____
_____
_____

However, many people would disagree with me and consider _____
_____
_____
_____
_____

An argument they might use to support them would be _____
_____
_____
_____
_____
_____

Word Bank

- nurture
- shared aims
- mission
- integration
- distinctive
- secular
- faith
- ethos
- inclusive
- community

FRAMEWORK RE 3

Worksheet 2.5

Use this worksheet to help you with Activity Two.

Task

Look at the sources of information about the Amish on pages 46–47 and any further information you have gained from websites. Then complete the writing frame below.

I didn't know that …
I was surprised at …
I disagree with …
I agree with …
I would like to find out more about …
I would like to ask the three following questions: 1. 2. 3.

UNIT 3: WHAT INSIGHTS DO DIFFERENT RELIGIONS BRING TO GOOD AND EVIL?

INTRODUCTION

The purpose of this unit is to develop pupils' knowledge and understanding of the key concepts of good and evil. It develops their understanding of how different religious traditions have considered the nature and purpose of suffering and evil, and applies religious beliefs to their own thinking. It enhances the conceptual development of pupils, both in terms of aspects of the religion themselves as well as towards aspects of life in general.

Contents

The unit consists of five lessons. It begins by exploring the role conscience plays when distinguishing between good and evil. This is built upon in the second lesson through the distinction between natural and moral evil. Different religious attitudes to evil are also explored. The third lesson focuses on the symbolic understanding of light within many religious traditions. The fourth lesson moves onto explore examples of good behaviour and practice in sacred scriptures, and gives opportunities to reflect upon role models in contemporary society. The unit concludes with different attitudes and beliefs concerning heaven. In all cases the general concepts are dealt with as well as some specific religious beliefs and practices to which they are related.

Appendices

- Appendix A: Record of achievement chart.
- Appendix B: Grid identifying the various learning styles, skills and methods employed in each lesson.

APPENDIX A

FRAMEWORK RE 3: RECORD OF ACHIEVEMENT
UNIT 3

PUPIL NAME: _____ GROUP: _____ TEACHER: _____

LESSON	AT1	AT1	AT2	AT2
	Activity	Mark	Activity	Mark
1	1		1	
	2		2	
			3	
	NTT			
2	1		1	
	2		2	
	NTT			
3	1			
	2			
			3	
			NTT	
4			1	
			2	
			3	
	NTT			
5	1			
	2		2	
	3		3	
			NTT	
LEVEL				

NOTES ON PROGRESS:

TARGETS:

Signed (Pupil) _____ Signed (Teacher) _____

APPENDIX B

UNIT 3: COVERAGE OF LEARNING ACTIVITIES, STYLES, METHODS, SKILLS

	Lesson 1	Lesson 2	Lesson 3	Lesson 4	Lesson 5
Classification		✖	✖	✖	
Most likely					
Odd one out					
Reveal					✖
Sequencing					
Show me					
Reflective questioning	✖	✖	✖	✖	✖
Multiple choice					✖
Ranking		✖		✖	
Drag and drop			✖		
Matching		✖			
Filling in gaps					
Writing	✖	✖	✖		
Brainstorming	✖		✖	✖	✖
Discussion	✖	✖	✖	✖	✖
Comparing	✖		✖	✖	✖
Investigating	✖				✖
Questioning	✖		✖	✖	✖
Explaining	✖	✖	✖	✖	✖
Giving accounts	✖				✖
Mind map			✖		
Evaluating	✖	✖		✖	✖
Imagining	✖		✖		✖
Analysing					
Synthesising	✖		✖		
Empathising	✖	✖			✖
Criticising					
Negotiating				✖	✖
Deciding		✖	✖	✖	
Expressing clearly	✖	✖	✖	✖	✖
Listening	✖	✖	✖	✖	✖
Interpreting	✖		✖		✖
Applying				✖	✖
Responding	✖	✖	✖	✖	✖
Observing	✖		✖		✖
Learning styles					
Kinaesthetic	✖		✖	✖	
Auditory				✖	
Visual	✖	✖	✖	✖	✖

1. HOW CAN PEOPLE TELL THE DIFFERENCE BETWEEN GOOD AND EVIL?

Pupil's Book pages 50–53

Aim
The aim of this lesson is to teach pupils the role of the conscience when making ethical decisions.

Learning objectives
By the end of the lesson pupils should have:
- thought about what we mean by conscience (AT1d, 2a and 2e)
- been able to express their own ideas about conscience (AT2c, 2d and 2e)
- understood why many Quakers are conscientious objectors (AT1e).

Skills involved
Pupils will be:
- thinking about differences between good and evil
- expressing ideas about the role of conscience
- finding out about conscientious objectors.

Information
There are many different views on the nature of conscience, although it is usually defined as a state in which a person really feels what they are truly like. A person's beliefs will be reflected in their understanding of conscience, although most would say that it takes effort to develop conscience. It is not the same as morality, which can vary according to different cultures and times. Conscience is permanent and acts as a guide to the way people act in the world. The study of conscience may lay a foundation for the study of Christian Ethics at GCSE.

The Religious Society of Friends, usually known as the Quakers, believes that war can never be justified. Although they recognise that there is evil, they do not believe it can be extinguished by using weapons. During wars they refuse to fight but will aim to be involved in other peaceful ways such as nursing. If appropriate, reference should be made to the fact that many Jehovah's Witnesses are conscientious objectors.

Use of ICT
Research: In Activity 3 part 1, pupils could use the stimulus provided in the Pupil's Book or research their own examples using the Internet.
Communication: In Activity 1 part 3, pupils could present their results using ICT. In Activity 2 part 3, pupils could use ICT to design the logo.

ICT Resource: See *Framework RE 3 ICT Resource* Teacher's Notes, page 52.

Activity 1 (AT2c)   Worksheet 3.1
Worksheet 3.1 could be used before the first activity as it requires pupils to distinguish between moral and immoral action. The worksheet presents a situation where pupils have to consider if the actions are moral or immoral. As they gather more information their views may well change.

Pupils should work in small groups of three or four and, before the worksheet activity begins, establish their criteria for making a group decision. The worksheet should be cut into strips. Each strip should be turned over and discussed one at a time to allow discussion. Pupils should be encouraged to raise questions about the situation described in each strip, for example, for the first strip a question could be 'Was the building inhabited?'. They then need to write their group decision on each strip.

Activity 1 encourages pupils to use visual skills to suggest meanings. The photos show the different ways that humans use their unique skills (going to the moon and genocide). Some pupils would be assisted by stating what they actually see in the pictures before trying to suggest a meaning. In the second part of the activity, for some pupils, it might be helpful to produce some titles that they have to select from and to justify their selection. The actual title given was, 'Human beings are capable of anything.' Possible titles could include:
- Which is best?
- How do humans use their skills?
- Which would God want?
- Why?
- When will we learn?

In the third part of the activity pupils could use a range of newspapers and magazines to give them examples for their collage. The examples used would reflect differentiation by outcome. Collages may include examples of kindness and cruelty; birth and death; harvest and tornados; etc.

Activity 2 (AT1d, AT2a and AT2c)
In this activity pupils are expected to use skills of critical analysis, discussion, interpretation and expression. In the first part of the activity many of the descriptions would be relevant for each of the quotes. They all agree that conscience is inner and tells us the sort of behaviour we should follow. Only Joseph Butler refers to it being the voice of God.

In the second part of the activity pupils should be challenged to consider the question 'If a conscience is not the voice of God then where does it come from?'.

The third part of the activity will particularly support visual learners. To help support some pupils the class could discuss:

- If conscience was a colour what would it be?
- If conscience was a shape would it be a circle, a square or a line?

Activity 3 (AT2d and AT2e)

In the first part of the activity pupils consider how the words of Martin Luther King relate to their own life experiences. Due to the sensitive nature of this activity pupils should be allowed to work on their own or in pairs.

The quote should be placed in the context of what pupils already know about Martin Luther King.

In the second part of the activity, pupils can work in pairs or groups to consider the effects of conscience. Expected answers may include:

- Equal rights – ordination of women.
- Animal rights – hunting/zoos.
- Sanctity of life – attitudes to abortion and euthanasia.

Again pupils could be encouraged to look through the Pupil's Book to give them support.

Now try this (extension work) (AT1e)

In the rewriting, pupils will have to use a range of technical terms, such as beliefs, truth and conviction, and to express insights into the relationships between beliefs and practices. Pupils can draw upon other teachings that were written a long time ago when they discuss the relevance of the Peace Testimony.

Suggestions for homework and follow-up work

1 Use the Internet to find out more about how Martin Luther King and Ghandi followed their conscience.
2 Use the Internet to explore Prisoners of Conscience on the Amnesty International website.

Framework RE 3 ICT Resource Teacher's Notes

Starter activity

Pupils can work in groups or independently for this activity. Each pupil or group should take it in turns to remove a piece of the jigsaw until they can guess what the picture is. They should then brainstorm the similarities and differences between the pictures. One picture is of a family and the other is of a lion and cubs.

Answers
The similarities might include:

- all are alive
- all need food
- children/cubs are looked after
- adults can kill
- all can communicate.

The differences might include:

- humans can talk
- lions cannot read
- humans have a sense of right and wrong
- humans have a conscience.

Through this activity pupils should become aware of the distinctive role of conscience that separates humans from the animal world.

Main activity

This activity gives pupils the opportunity to reflect upon their own moral code. It requires them to identify where their own conscience is a directive factor, not the moral code of parents, schools or peers. Pupils can then share their responses to produce a graph or pie chart to illustrate whether their moral conscience has arisen because of:

- previous experience
- what they have read
- rational thought
- influences of others.

Plenary activity

Pupils should be split into teams to work out the anagrams in less than two minutes. The anagrams are key terms that have been used in the lesson. Some pupils/teams can then progress to the next screen by clicking on the arrow at the bottom, to try to use four of the terms in a sentence. Again they have two minutes to do this.

Answers

1 Ethics
2 Immoral
3 Moral
4 Conscience
5 Conscientious objectors
6 Society of Friends

Example of a sentence
Many members of the Society of Friends are conscientious objectors because their conscience tells them that war is immoral.

2. WHY IS THERE EVIL?

Pupil's Book pages 54–57

Aim

The aim of this lesson is to investigate the nature of evil by reflecting on three different teachings.

Learning objectives

By the end of the lesson pupils should have:
- thought about what we mean by evil (AT1g and 2a)
- gained an understanding of two religious attitudes to evil (AT1e)
- reflected upon their own views concerning the nature of evil (AT1h and 2e).

Skills involved

Pupils will be:
- reflecting upon the difference between natural and moral evil
- investigating Hindu, Humanist and Christian teaching on evil
- thinking about how and why evil behaviour occurs.

Information

Many religious people believe that although they have been created by God they have been given free will in which humans have free choices in life and are responsible for their actions. For Christians and Jews this belief can be found in the story of Adam and Eve in the book of Genesis in the Bible. Adam and Eve chose to eat the fruit of the tree of knowledge of good and evil. As a result they were thrown out of Eden and made to take responsibility for their actions.

This lesson may lead into a wider study of ethics and a discussion about different types of morality, such as the idea that as human beings we will all have a different sense of what is right and wrong.
- Absolute morality – someone who is an absolute moralist always follows the rules.
- Relative morality – someone who is an relative moralist tries to judge a situation before making a decision.

Use of ICT

Research: To use the Internet to find further information on the beliefs contained in this lesson, or on the attitudes of other religions towards evil.
Communication: The Venn diagram in Activity 2 could be produced using ICT. The answers to Worksheet 3.3 could be presented using ICT skills.

ICT Resource: See *Framework RE 3 ICT Resource Teacher's Notes*, page 54.

Activity 1 (AT1e, AT1f and AT2a)

The starter activity is designed to make pupils aware of the different types of evil that exist. In their categorisation they will realise that some acts of evil are both moral and natural. For each picture they are expected to suggest reasons as to why this evil occurred.

Answers:
1. Could be an example of natural or moral evil. The natural disaster (famine) some would say has been caused by moral evil (apathy from the western world; corrupt politics; people not caring for the environment)
2. Natural evil
3. Moral evil
4. Deforestation can be seen as a natural evil but the impact of human actions might be referred to
5. Moral evil.

With more able students their group discussions could lead to an exploration of the role of science and God. Pupils are expected to reflect on their own view of what an evil act is. It may not be appropriate to share these with the rest of the class.

Now try this (extension work) (AT1e)

Teachers can either direct pupils to the two traditions they need to explore, or allow pupils to make the selection. Distinguishing differences and similarities in a graphic form will support visual learners. It is important that pupils recognise that these would not be the views of all Hindus, Humanists or Christians.

Activity 2 (AT1g and AT2e) Worksheet 3.2

This activity requires pupils to interpret a range of texts and sources regarding the nature of evil and to express their own beliefs and ideas. The quotes could be displayed throughout different areas of the classroom and pupils could stand by the quote they least agree with and as a group decide on a justification. Worksheet 3.2 allows pupils to highlight their choices.

Suggestions for homework and follow-up work Worksheet 3.3

Pupils do not have to conduct the survey on Worksheet 3.3, although it would give them experience of a wider range of views. The purpose of the worksheet is to be able to identify, select and justify their choice of relevant questions. It could be completed using ICT.

Framework RE 3 ICT Resource Teacher's Notes

Starter activity

This activity asks pupils to classify certain actions into whether they think they are 'Evil', 'Bad' or 'Neither good nor bad' by dragging and dropping them into the appropriate columns in the table. Although the judgements cannot be finite, pupils should be able to reflect upon the different attributes that make an act 'evil'. A class consensus on the classifications could then be carried out. This classification and the discussion that results can lead into a question about the nature of evil and whether there are any common features of the actions they classified as evil. The results of this activity will be used in the main ICT activity.

Main activity

In this activity pupils are presented with a series of statements that relate to an action where harm has been done. Pupils should decide how strongly they agree or disagree with whether each statement makes the act evil or not. There are eight statements in total, one on each screen. Click on the arrow at the bottom of the screen to go on to the next.

When categorising whether these criteria make an action evil or not, pupils could test the statements against different events in the past, for example the Soham murders, the tsunami, an example of animal cruelty, the Holocaust. There will be a variety of answers, although most will relate to evil intent and the vulnerability of the victim(s). Pupils should be expected to justify their selection using relevant examples and identify the criteria they used in defining acts as evil. This activity could be completed through independent learning although the issue can be discussed as a class.

Plenary activity

In pairs, pupils have to answer four questions. They are allowed ten seconds to answer each. As this is against a time allowance, pupils need to have considered how they will agree on an answer. There are four questions in total, one on each screen. Click on the arrow at the bottom of the screen to go to the next.

Answers

1	Moral/moral evil	3	Ignorance
2	Job/Book of Job	4	Evil

3. HOW IS LIGHT USED AS A SYMBOL?

Pupil's Book pages 58–61

Aim

The aim of this lesson is to teach pupils that a range of religions use light as a symbol of good.

Learning objectives

By the end of the lesson pupils should have:

- gained an understanding of religious beliefs about the symbolic nature of light (AT1b)
- thought about how light is used in religious and secular rituals and teachings (AT1b and 1g)
- expressed their own ideas about light as a symbol using a variety of expressions (AT2e)
- gained an understanding of religious beliefs about the symbolic nature of light (AT1b and 2d).

Skills involved

Pupils will be:

- identifying how light is used as a symbol in religious teachings and rituals
- finding out the importance of light in many religions
- expressing their own ideas about the symbol of light.

Use of ICT

Research: To use the Internet to find further information on the beliefs and practices contained in this lesson, or on the attitudes of religious people towards light and enlightenment.

Communication: Pupils could use ICT to produce a concept map for the second part of Activity 1 and Activity 3 and to present their findings in Activity 2.

ICT Resource: See *Framework RE 3 ICT Resource Teacher's Notes,* page 55.

Activity 1 (AT1b and AT1g)

This starter activity is designed to provoke discussion and recap on prior learning.

The focus of the activity is the range of different ways light is used in religious ceremonies and rituals. The importance of this exercise is the way pupils use prior learning in their justifications. Pupils may refer to the following in their answers:

1 f) As a mark of remembrance and hope.
2 g) As a mark of time for preparation leading up to Christmas. Some pupils may refer that the candle is also symbolic of the duality of Christ with the divine becoming human.
3 b) and/or a) and/or f) There are many purposes for lighting divas. Some would say to celebrate a happy time; a welcoming for Lakshmi; a sign of remembrance of Rama and Sita.
4 b) and/or f) To celebrate a happy time. Might also be referred to as a symbol of remembrance (of birth) and hope (for the future).
5 c) and/or e) An act of Prayer and devotion. Some might also refer to the dual nature of Christ.
6 d) As a source of guidance.
7 f) As a mark of remembrance and hope.

Pupils can work in groups to produce their answers to part 2. Some higher ability pupils could use ICT to create a concept map. Answers may include:

- in places of worship or to signify the existence of God, for example, the ner tamid
- to give light in darkness, for example, a torch
- as a title, for example, The Buddha or Enlightened One.

The ICT Activity on *Framework RE 3 ICT Resource* provides an opportunity for further discussion concerning the pictures and a word bank to support and extend different abilities.

Activity 2 (AT1b)
Pupils are asked to read through the information and then analyse the symbolic nature of light in each of the teachings. The table should reflect that although light has been used in each of the traditions it has a range of different significances, for example, in Islam it is used to symbolise a quality of Allah; in Hinduism light is used to refer to a wisdom that all can achieve. The results of the table will distinguish the practice (how it is used) from the associated belief (why).

Activity 3 (AT2d and AT2e)   Worksheet 3.4
In the first part of the activity pupils create a spider diagram or concept map showing the different concepts light symbolises. Pupils should identify a variety of examples from different religious and secular life stances, for example, celebration could include birthday candles (secular), Divas (religious), fireworks (secular). More able pupils could be asked to identify whether each of their examples is secular or religious.

The second part of the activity asks pupils to rewrite a famous saying and therefore to draw out its meaning. The quote points out that everyone can do something to conquer evil or to make a positive difference. This is further developed by Worksheet 3.4, which asks pupils to consider a person (famous on not) who 'lights their darkness'. There is a writing frame to support some pupils. The completed worksheets and justifications could be used as a wall display.

Now try this (extension work) (AT2e)
Pupils can choose their preferred learning style to express the quote by Martin Luther King. If time allows, pupils could produce a collage of their pictures and stories.

Framework RE 3 ICT Resource Teacher's Notes

Starter activity
The pictures from this activity are on pages 58–59 of the Pupil's Book. Pupils are expected to write their own captions to the pictures, using words from the word bank. This activity allows teachers to assess any misconceptions, and pupils' understanding of some key concepts. There are seven pictures in total, one on each screen. Click on the arrow at the bottom of the screen to move on to the next.

Possible matches with key words might be:

	symbol	ritual	Jesus	Divali	Hindu	secular	Christian
Picture 1	✓	✓				✓	
Picture 2	✓	✓	✓				✓
Picture 3	✓	✓		✓	✓		
Picture 4	✓	✓				✓	✓
Picture 5	✓	✓					
Picture 6	✓					✓	
Picture 7	✓	✓				✓	

Main activity

Pupils should look at the clues and then enter the answers in the crossword grid. Pupils will use many of the key terms from this lesson in their crossword and it will necessitate them using the correct spellings.

Answers

Across answers

1 Bhagavad Gita

2 Hargobind

3 Jesus

4 Hinduism

Down answers

5 Allah

6 Hanukkah

7 Christianity

8 Knowledge

Plenary activity

This activity gives an opportunity for stilling. It may be appropriate for one pupil to read the poem or for pupils to read it in silence. Either a time allowance should be given or a piece of appropriate music could be played.

Further examples might include: old without young, learning without ignorance, belief without knowledge.

4. HOW DO WE LEARN FROM OUR ROLE MODELS?

Pupil's Book pages 62–65

Aim

The aim of this lesson is to encourage pupils to recognise there are many different influential characteristics of role models and to understand the importance of Krishna for many Hindus.

Learning objectives

By the end of the lesson pupils should have:
- identified key features of role models (AT2e)
- interpreted a range of sources to consider qualities of Krishna's life (AT1g)
- analysed the significance of Krishna for many Hindus (AT1a)
- explained what and who inspires and influences them (AT2c).

Skills involved

Pupils will be:
- identifying the different features of role models
- interpreting a range of sources to understand the significance of Krishna for many Hindus
- reflecting upon the people who inspire and influence them.

Information

The information in this lesson is presented in a series of different visual and written sources. It is hoped that pupils can investigate the different pictures and stories to ascertain a range of attributes of role models.

Krishna is the most popular avatar of Vishnu and there are many stories that can be explored to show his courage (for example, when Krishna fought the demons), his mischief (for example, when Krishna stole the butter milk) and his care for others (for example, when Krishna saved a village). When George Harrison became a devotee of Krishna he wrote many songs which reflected his religious beliefs. One of these was *My Sweet Lord*.

While the activities are being completed the song could be played and a murti of Krishna placed as a focal point in the classroom.

A visit to Bhaktivedanta Manor near Watford would support pupils in their knowledge and understanding of Krishna to many Hindus.

Use of ICT

Research: To find out more examples of role models and how their words and actions are inspirational. To explore how respect is shown on Martin Luther King Day. Activity

3 and the 'Now try this' activity can be supported by investigating the websies: www.iskcon.com and www.Hindunet.org.

Communication: For Activity 2, pupils could scan in the outline of Krishna and use ICT to complete the activity.

ICT Resource: See *Framework RE 3 ICT Resource* Teacher's Notes (below).

Activity 1 (AT2c and AT2e)

This first activity raises the awareness that there are different attributes of role models such as actions, attitudes, courage, skill and teachings. A range of religious and non-religious people are used as examples. Expected answers would be:

1 inspirational actions
2 wise teachings
3 commitment; dedication; skill and determination
4 commitment; courage; skill and determination
5 skill and determination; dedication.

The third part of the activity allows pupils to reflect upon their own different role models and to justify their own selections.

Activity 2 (AT1g)   **Worksheets 3.5 and 3.6**

By using a range of different written and visual sources pupils investigate the different actions and qualities of Krishna and present their findings in pictorial form. Worksheet 3.5 provides support in the form of a word bank for any pupils who find it difficult to read through the text.

The second part of the activity asks pupils to consider which is more important – whether Krishna lived or the impact of his teachings and actions.

Worksheet 3.6 contains the lyrics of *My Sweet Lord*. Pupils are asked to underline (or highlight) words that show how Krishna is respected.

Activity 3 (AT2e)

Pupils can discuss and share with their partners how they show respect to their role models. Answers may include putting posters in their bedroom; reading about them; trying to visit places associated with them; trying to copy features of their lives or personalities; etc.

Now try this (extension work) (AT1a)

Some pupils should be able to make connections with previous learning. From the quote pupils should be able to deduce the all-embracing effect of Krishna in thought; actions and worship. Using websites such as www.hindunet.org and www.iskcon.com will give further examples such as Janmashtami; fasts; special clothes made for the murtis; chanting Krishna's name; etc.

Suggestions for homework and follow-up work

1 Explore how Martin Luther King Day is celebrated.
2 Conduct a survey to show influential qualities in role models.

Framework RE 3 ICT Resource Teacher's Notes

Starter activity

This activity asks pupils to categorise different qualities a role model could have by deciding whether they are 'not important', 'quite important' or 'very important' and dragging and dropping them into the appropriate columns. In deciding how to categorise them, discussion could focus on the effect of those qualities on others and how long the qualities may last. To round off the activity, pupils could decide which attribute they consider the most important. This activity should support Activity Two in the Pupil's Book (page 65) when pupils are reflecting upon the characteristics of Krishna.

Main activity

In this activity pupils are asked to decide how strongly they agree or disagree with different statements about role models.

You could organise this activity by placing pupils in groups that reflect their response (so, for example, all the 'strongly agrees' are put together) and ask them to negotiate a group justification.

Responses may include:

● We often hear the bad news and not about all the good acts people do.

● References to particular individuals, for example Bono or people within the community.

● No one can be perfect but people can do individual good actions.

● Pop stars should realise the influence they have on people.

● The way that Jesus showed concern for others is important to everyone to follow.

There are three statements in total, one on each screen. Click on the arrow at the bottom of the screen to move on to the next.

Plenary activity

In this activity you could organise the pupils into teams to compete to solve the anagrams first. In the feedback, in addition to solving the anagram, you could ask them to give a definition of each word. It is important for pupils to pronounce each of the words as this will support their development of religious literacy. Some pupils may be able to use all the words in a paragraph describing what they have learned in the lesson.

Answers

1 Krishna

2 Vrindavan

3 Hindu

4 Bhagavad Gita

5 Role model

6 Karma

5. WHAT ATTITUDES DO PEOPLE HAVE TO HEAVEN?

Pupil's Book pages 66–69

Aim

The aim of the lesson is to teach pupils that there are many different views concerning the existence and nature of heaven.

Learning objectives

By the end of the lesson pupils should have:

- investigated and interpreted a range of different stimuli (AT1g)
- been able to sort and categorise views about heaven (AT1d)
- been able to reflect on and express their own views about the nature of heaven (AT2a and 2e)
- gained knowledge and understanding of a range of beliefs about heaven (AT1a and 1e).

Skills involved

Pupils will be:

- interpreting a picture to investigate different views about heaven
- finding out different beliefs concerning heaven
- reflecting on and expressing their own ideas about heaven.

Additional information

In July 1999 Pope John Paul II declared that heaven is not a place above the clouds where angels play harps but simply a state of being after death. Just as hell is being separate from God so heaven is the reverse.

Use of ICT

Research: To develop answers on Worksheet 3.7, further information on faith teachings could be obtained from websites such as www.tolerance.org or www.bbc.religions.org.

Communication: Pupils could use ICT to present their findings from the homework activity.

ICT Resource: See *Framework RE 3 ICT Resource Teacher's Notes*, page 59.

Activity 1 (AT1g) Worksheet 3.7

In this starter activity pupils should explore the picture – particularly focusing on the use of symbols and interpretations by the French book illustrator Gustave Dore (1832–83). Reference should be made to the fact that although there are teachings about heaven in all the world faiths, the members of each faith community will have different views and interpretations.

In the second part of the activity pupils should suggest answers to the questions. Each pair could suggest an answer which is then, along with the other pairs' answers, put to a class vote.

The poem on Worksheet 3.7 could be read at the beginning of the lesson and images used in the poem could be compared with those seen in the picture by Dore.

Activity 2 (AT1d, AT1g and AT2e)

In the first part of this activity pupils consider a range of statements concerning the nature of heaven. Pupils are asked to categorise them into those that argue:

- there is no heaven
- heaven is a real place
- heaven is a state of mind.

Some pupils may be able to suggest faith and non-faith traditions associated with some of the statements.

In the second part of the activity pupils draw or design their own views. The use of colour and symbols will be particularly significant.

Activity 3 (AT1a, AT1b and AT1e)

Worksheet 3.7

From the information pupils are asked to identify which traditions would agree with certain statements.

Pupils should be aware that although Hindus believe in moksha it is not the same as the Christian/Islamic concept of heaven. Answers should include:

a) Christianity, Islam, Baha'i
b) Christianity, Islam, Baha'i
c) Islam, Baha'i
d) Humanists.

The activity on Worksheet 3.7 requires pupils to use their knowledge and understanding of faith perspectives to answer the questions in the poem. Websites such as www.bbc.religions.org or www.tolerance.org could be used for further research.

Now try this (extension work) (AT2a)

In this activity pupils will need to consider appropriate choice of questions, which would move their learning on and so support independent learning. This activity could be done in groups so that pupils have to justify the questions they want asked and analyse which would be the best.

Suggestions for homework and follow-up work

1 Interview five people of different ages and ask them the following questions:
   - Does heaven exist and if so what is it like?
   - Have you always held that view?
   - If not, when and why did your view change?

2 Present the results from your interviews.

Framework RE 3 ICT Resource Teacher's Notes

Starter activity

Pupils should be asked to reveal the jigsaw pieces until they can guess what the image underneath is. As each piece is removed pupils must make a justified guess about what the picture shows.

Main activity

This activity is to get pupils to consider and interpret information. They are presented with a series of statistics from a poll of 8000 people to investigate whether they believe in an afterlife. This poll was carried out in 2005. The pupils then have a series of four statements to which, using the statistics alone, they must attribute the answer 'yes', 'no' or 'don't know'. Each statement is on a separate screen. Click on the arrow at the bottom of the screen to move on to the next.

Suggested answers
In their justifications pupils may respond as follows:

1 Don't know – Poland has more people who believe in an afterlife but that does not mean they are Christians.

2 Yes – the European average is 53 per cent.

3 Don't know – there is nothing in the statistics to support this view.

4 Don't know – many people believe in an afterlife, but not necessarily in heaven.

Plenary activity

Pupils should be split into teams to work out the anagrams in less than two minutes. The anagrams are key terms that have been used in the lesson. Some pupils/teams can then progress to the next screen by clicking on the arrow at the bottom, to try to use three of the terms in a sentence. Again they have two minutes to do this.

Answers

1 Day of Judgement
2 Heaven
3 Moksha
4 Reincarnation
5 Paradise
6 Humanists
7 Christians
8 Hindus
9 Islam

Examples of a sentence

● Many Muslims believe that the Day of Judgement will decide who goes to Paradise.

● Hindus don't believe in a Paradise or Heaven as they believe in reincarnation.

FRAMEWORK RE 3

Worksheet 3.1

Use this worksheet to help you with Activity One.

Task

After you have read each statement decide with your group if the action is a moral or immoral action. Keep a note of the reason behind your decision.

---

1. A person smashes a window and breaks into a building.
Moral or immoral?
Why?

---

2. The building he has broken into is an animal testing laboratory.
Moral or immoral?
Why?

---

3. As he enters the building he sprays gas in someone's face.
Moral or immoral?
Why?

---

4. He takes the animals that are held there and takes them to good caring homes.
Moral or immoral?
Why?

---

5. He steals £700 and gives it to an animal charity.
Moral or immoral?
Why?

---

6. He destroys all the research equipment and the results of the animal experimentation.
Moral or immoral?
Why?

FRAMEWORK RE 3

Worksheet 3.2

Use this worksheet to help you with Activity Two.

Albert Einstein

The world is a dangerous place to live, not because of the people who are evil, but because of the people who don't do anything about it.

Martin Luther King

Whoever accepts evil without protesting against it is really co-operating with it.

Edmund Burke

It is necessary only for the good to do nothing for evil to happen.

Epicurus

If God exists, is good, loving and all powerful why does he let evil happen?

Swami Vivekananda

We have no theory of evil. We call it ignorance.

The Bible *1 Timothy 6 v.10*

Love of money is the root of all evil.

The Bible *Job 18:21*

Evil comes to those who do evil ... people get what they deserve.

FRAMEWORK RE 3

Worksheet 3.3

Use this worksheet to help you with your homework.

Task

A research company has asked you to write an article explaining the beliefs about evil in your community. As part of this activity you will have to conduct a survey of six people who will give a wide range of viewpoints. Which community will you use? School? Family? Hobby? Worshipping?

For your survey you are allowed to ask three of the following questions. Which three will you select and do you think they will give further support for your research?

Do you believe in God?		Why?
Why do you think evil exists?		Why?
Is there more evil now than in the last century?		Why?
How can there be a god if evil exists?		Why?
Does the devil exist?		Why?
Have your views on evil changed and why?		Why?
Can evil ever be stopped?		Why?

Identify which six people you will ask and why you think they will help your research. Remember you need to get a wide range of views.

1 _____

Why? _____

2 _____

Why? _____

3 _____

Why? _____

4 _____

Why? _____

5 _____

Why? _____

6 _____

Why? _____

FRAMEWORK RE 3

Worksheet 3.4

Use this worksheet to help you with Activity Three.

Task

In everyone's life there is someone in their community who 'lights their darkness'. Consider who that person is for you. You do not have to name them.

In the stem of the candle write why and how they 'light your darkness'. Look back at the words you have identified as the symbolic meaning of light and select the appropriate words for your flame.

FRAMEWORK RE 3

Worksheet 3.5

Use this worksheet to help you with Activity Two.

1.   Place words that relate to Krishna's qualities inside the silhouette and those that relate to external features of his life on the outside. The word bank gives you a starting point.

2.   Find some other stories about Krishna in books or on the Internet and add some more examples to your silhouette.

Word Bank

- killed Kaliya
- people trusted him
- gave advice to Arjuna

- can overcome evil
- picked up Mount Goverdhan with his little finger
- taught the importance of karma and doing one's duty

- a leader

- brave
- wise teacher
- responsible

FRAMEWORK RE 3

Worksheet 3.6

Use this worksheet to help you with Activity Two.

Task

Underline the key words which show how Krishna is considered a role model.

Lyrics for *My Sweet Lord* by George Harrison

My sweet lord, my lord, mm my lord
I really want to see you
Really want to be with you
Really want to see you lord
But it takes so long my lord
My sweet lord, mm my lord
Mm my lord

I really want to know you
Really want to go with you
Really want to show you lord
That it won't take long – my lord

(hallelulah)
My sweet lord
(hallelulah)
Mm my lord
(hallelulah)
My sweet lord
(hallelulah)

I really want to see you
Really want to see you
Really want to see you lord
Really want to see you lord
But it takes so long my lord

(hallelulah)
My sweet lord
(hallelulah)
Mm my lord
(hallelulah)
My my my lord
(hallelulah)
I really want to know you
(hallelulah)
Really want to go with you
(hallelulah)
Really want to show you lord
That it won't take long
(hallelulah)

Worksheet 3.6 (continued)

Mmmmmmmm
(hallelulah)
My sweet lord
(hallelulah)
My my lord

Mmm my lord
(Hare Krishna)
My my my lord
(Hare Krishna)

My my sweet lord
Krishna Krishna
My lord
Hare Hare
Now I really want to see you
Hare Rama
Really want to be
Hare Rama
Really want to see you lord
But it takes so long my lord
(hallelulah)
Ooo lord
(hallelulah)
My my lord
Hare Krishna
My sweet lord
Hare Krishna
My sweet lord
Krishna Krishna
My sweet lord
Hare Hare
Mmmm

Guru Brahma
Guru Vishnu
Guru Devo
Maheshwar
My sweet lord
Guru Saksha
My sweet lord
Param Brahma
My my my lord
Tas Mai Shri
My my my my lord
Guru Vey Namah
My sweet lord
Hare Rama
Hare Krishna
Hare Krishna
My sweet lord

FRAMEWORK RE 3

Worksheet 3.7

Use this worksheet to help you with Activities One and Three.

Task

Read this poem by Steve Turner. Select one religious tradition and try to answer each question from that tradition's point of view. Further information can be found on the websites www.bbc.co.uk/religion and www.tolerance.org.

Heaven

What happens in heaven?
Will I sit on a cloud?
Is walking or talking or jumping allowed?

Will I be on my own
Or with some of my friends?
Does it go on for ever
Or eventually end?

What happens in heaven?
Will I play a harp's strings?
I can't play piano
I can't even sing.

Who chooses the music
That angels inspire?
Who does the auditions
For the heavenly choir?

What happens in heaven?
Are the streets paved with gold?
Is it crowded with people
Who're incredibly old?

Will I know who I am?
Will I know what I'm called?
If I pinch myself hard
Will I feel it at all?

What happens in heaven?
Do I go through a gate?
What if I get myself lost
Or turn up too late?

Is my name on a list?
Is the gatekeeper nice?
Can you sneak in for nothing
Or is there a price?

UNIT 4: WHAT DO RELIGIONS SAY ABOUT THE USE OF MONEY AND OTHER RESOURCES?

INTRODUCTION

The purpose of this unit is to allow pupils to consider the impact of religious and non-religious beliefs on wealth and resources. It develops their skills of working out the impact of being religious and the application of aspects of religious beliefs to their own thinking. The unit therefore also develops pupils' skills of interpreting and applying their learning to life today, and so covers some of the required themes of the Framework.

Contents

The unit begins with a consideration of different attitudes to wealth. The second lesson builds on this by focusing on religious teachings concerning ways of gaining wealth and the impact of these teachings for daily life. The third lesson moves to consider the attitude of Christianity and Islam to looking after the Earth's resources. This is developed in the fourth lesson by particularly focusing on the attitude to animals. The unit ends with opportunities for pupils to reflect upon many different spiritual qualities through their own lives and through specific case studies.

Appendices

- Appendix A: Record of achievement chart.
- Appendix B: Grid identifying the various learning styles, skills and methods employed in each lesson.

APPENDIX A

FRAMEWORK RE 3: RECORD OF ACHIEVEMENT
UNIT 4

PUPIL NAME: _____ GROUP: _____ TEACHER: _____

LESSON	AT1 Activity	AT1 Mark	AT2 Activity	AT2 Mark
1	1			
			2	
			NTT	
2	1		1	
			2	
	3			
	NTT			
3			1	
			2	
			3	
			NTT	
4	1		1	
5			1	
	2		2	
	3		3	
			NTT	
6	1			
			2	
			3	
	NTT		NTT	
LEVEL				

NOTES ON PROGRESS:

TARGETS:

Signed (Pupil) _____ Signed (Teacher) _____

APPENDIX B

UNIT 4: COVERAGE OF LEARNING ACTIVITIES, STYLES, METHODS, SKILLS

	Lesson 1	Lesson 2	Lesson 3	Lesson 4	Lesson 5	Lesson 6
Classification	✖				✖	
Most likely		✖				
Odd one out				✖	✖	
Reveal			✖			
Sequencing					✖	✖
Show me						
Reflective questioning	✖	✖	✖	✖	✖	✖
Multiple choice						
Ranking		✖				
Drag and drop			✖			✖
Matching	✖	✖				✖
Filling in gaps						
Writing	✖	✖	✖	✖	✖	✖
Brainstorming	✖	✖	✖	✖	✖	✖
Discussion	✖	✖	✖	✖	✖	✖
Comparing	✖	✖	✖		✖	
Investigating					✖	
Questioning	✖	✖	✖			
Explaining	✖	✖	✖	✖	✖	✖
Giving accounts			✖			
Mind map						
Evaluating		✖		✖	✖	✖
Imagining	✖	✖	✖	✖	✖	
Analysing				✖	✖	✖
Synthesising						
Empathising		✖	✖	✖	✖	✖
Criticising						
Negotiating						
Deciding	✖	✖	✖	✖	✖	✖
Expressing clearly	✖	✖	✖	✖	✖	✖
Listening	✖	✖	✖	✖	✖	✖
Interpreting	✖		✖	✖		
Applying		✖				
Responding	✖	✖	✖	✖	✖	✖
Observing	✖				✖	✖
Learning styles						
Kinaesthetic						
Auditory		✖	✖		✖	
Visual	✖		✖	✖	✖	✖

1. WHAT IS THE RELIGIOUS ATTITUDE TO WEALTH?

Pupil's Book pages 72–75

Aim
The aim of this lesson is to teach pupils to investigate and reflect on the religious beliefs about the importance of wealth.

Learning objectives
By the end of the lesson pupils should have:
- gained a knowledge and understanding of religious attitudes to wealth (AT1a and 1b)
- reflected on and expressed ideas about the importance of wealth (AT2d and 2e)
- been able to interpret a range of religious and spiritual sources concerning wealth, contentment and materialism (AT1h).

Skills involved
Pupils will be:
- thinking about the importance of wealth
- identifying key beliefs about wealth from religious texts
- interpreting a range of sources concerning wealth and materialism.

Information
The information in this lesson incorporates some key terms, such as need, want and materialism, which pupils should become aware of and begin to use in their answers throughout this unit. This will support further study for GCSE.

Throughout this lesson a range of different sources are used. More able pupils should be made aware of the context of these and incorporate the implications into their answers. Pupils should be made particularly aware of:
- Mahabharata Shavi Parva
- Hadith
- Ethics of the Fathers
- Dhammapada
- Cakkatti Sidhananda Sutta.

In the second activity pupils are expected to reflect upon a story by Father Anthony De Mello who died in June 1987 in India. De Mello wrote five books which were all based on how to wake up and live. He maintained that most people needed to wake up and open their eyes to what is real inside and outside of themselves. He thought it was important for people to be in touch with themselves, their body, mind, feelings, thoughts and sensations.

Use of ICT
Research: To find out details about people who have used their money to help others in the local or global community.

Communication: The follow-up task could be produced using ICT and downloading and scanning appropriate images and examples.

ICT Resource: See *Framework RE 3 ICT Resource Teacher's Notes*, page 73.

Activity 1 (AT1a, AT1b and AT1h)
Worksheet 4.1
After completing the starter activity about contemporary society's attitudes towards wealth, in the second part of this activity pupils are expected to analyse the meanings of the sacred texts and place them into suitable categories. In this way pupils should be aware of the similar attitudes towards wealth held by many religions.

The three quotes draw out a particular concept concerning wealth:

a) Wealth holds importance only for life on earth.
b) The transitory nature of wealth.
c) The importance of personal qualities rather than wealth.

These three concepts are in contrast to the headlines extolling materialism in the first part of the activity.

Worksheet 4.1 instructs the pupils to highlight or cut out and sort the texts thereby allowing kinaesthetic development. Pupils will recognise that many religions share the same teachings concerning wealth, although they may use distinctive terminology, for example, maya.

In the third part of the activity pupils have to suggest a further view that two religions agree on. Examples could be:
- the importance of sharing wealth (Christianity and Hinduism)
- richness of the soul is more important than material wealth (Islam and Judaism).

In the final part of the activity pupils have to identify the impact of religious teachings on a believer's lifestyle. Pupils could be placed into groups to consider different areas, for example, the gaining of wealth; jobs; attitudes to charity; etc.

Activity 2 (AT2d and AT2e)
This is an open-ended activity in which pupils are asked to suggest meanings. The actual ending of the story is 'What do you think I am doing now?' but pupils may consider a range of endings and titles which will link with the religious teachings they have investigated. Reference may also be

made to the life of Socrates who would visit a market daily just to acknowledge what he was happy living without.

In the third part of the activity pupils could refer to a range of newspapers and magazines to help their discussions.

Now try this (extension work) (AT2e)

Pupils have to make their selection employing the concept of service rather than wealth. Connections could be made to the work in Unit 2 Lessons 2 and 3. The justifications should include reasoning and examples to show values and commitment through service.

Suggestions for homework and follow-up work

Collect pictures and examples of how people have used their wealth for good. These should be used to form a collage. Select one of the religious teachings to write in your collage. Be prepared to justify your selection to the class.

Framework RE 3 ICT Resource Teacher's Notes

Starter activity

The findings from the ICT Starter Activity support all the activities in the Pupil's Book (pages 72–75). As the correct findings are revealed, the teacher can prompt subsequent questions, such as:

a) Would spending bring contentment?

b) Is it fair?

There are five questions in total, one on each screen. Click on the arrow at the bottom of the screen to go on to the next.

Answers

1 d) £150

2 b) £140

3 a) So that their children didn't feel deprived.

4 a) True (A study by Beth Egan of the Social Market Foundation showed that those with an annual income below £5000 gave 4.5 per cent to charity but those earning more than £40,000 give just over 2 per cent.)

5 d) 57 per cent

Main activity

The purpose of this activity is for pupils to recognise that wealth does not provide all the necessities of life. Pupils sort the list into needs and wants by dragging and dropping them into the appropriate columns. There are no correct answers but pupils should be able to justify their choices. Most pupils will recognise that

there are examples of universal needs, for example somewhere to live, but that the type of place would depend on whether it is a need or a want.

The second screen, which has a quote from Socrates and asks pupils what they could be happy living without, can be used for some pupils to extend their thinking skills. Click on the arrows at the bottom to move between screens.

Plenary activity

This activity gives pupils the opportunity to engage with a range of religious texts and consolidates their learning from the first lesson. They are asked to explain the quotes in their own words and then match them to a picture or newspaper headline that illustrates what the quote could represent.

There are five quotes in total, one on each screen. Click on the arrow at the bottom of the screen to go on to the next.

Answers

1 Picture d

2 Picture c

3 Picture b

4 Picture a

5 Picture e

2. WHAT DO RELIGIONS SAY ABOUT WAYS OF GAINING WEALTH?

Pupil's Book pages 76–79

Aim

The aim of this lesson is to teach pupils about the range of religious and ethical issues when considering how money can be made.

Learning objectives

By the end of the lesson pupils should have:

- understood what Buddhists mean by right livelihood (AT1e)
- evaluated the importance of business ethics (AT2d)
- gained a knowledge and understanding of the teachings of Islam and The Society of Friends concerning gambling (AT1a)
- considered their own views on social and environmental issues (AT1h and 2c).

Skills involved

Pupils will be:

- recognising the role of ethics in businesses
- comparing Muslim and Quaker attitudes to gambling
- understanding why some religions don't approve of gambling.

Use of ICT

Research: To find out the range of environmental and social issues that The Body Shop has supported, www.uk.thebodyshop.com.

Communication: To present the situation when someone has made 'money their God' from the 'Now try this' activity as a story or newspaper article.

ICT Resource: See *Framework RE 3 ICT Resource* Teacher's Notes, page 75.

Information

This lesson uses The Body Shop as an example of business ethics. The Body Shop's mission statement opens with 'To dedicate our business to the pursuit of social and environmental change'.

There are many other local and national businesses which pupils could explore. In this lesson there would be opportunities to invite local businesses to discuss with pupils their particular business ethics and whether their motivation is a religious or secular one.

Activity 1 (AT1e, AT2c and AT2d)

The first part of the activity requires pupils to connect with previous learning on Buddhism. The Five Precepts have been included as a point of reference.

Pupils should be challenged to consider the wider aspects of each of the precepts for daily life. Answers may include the following:

a) Selling alcohol is not the same as drinking alcohol but it could be against the precept of not harming other living things.
b) No obvious moral dilemmas.
c) No obvious moral dilemmas.
d) Selling cigarettes is not the same as smoking them but it could be against the precept of not harming other living things.
e) Could go against the precept of not harming living things.
f) Could go against the precept of not harming living things.

Further considerations would include the way one does one's job could go against any of the precepts. For example, harming people through speech or action.

In the second part of the activity pupils may introduce to their discussion a range of viewpoints, for example, whether it is causing harm to others (physically or emotionally); whether it is harming the environment; or whether it is exploiting others, etc.

Activity 2 (AT2d)

This activity requires pupils to use their understanding of business ethics. This task will support pupils' skills for GCSE. The website www.uk.thebodyshop.com could be used to find out the range of environmental and social issues that The Body Shop has supported. These include campaigns connected with human rights, environmental issues, community trade and animal testing. In the second part of the activity pupils could look through the Pupil's Book for examples of campaigns they might choose.

Activity 3 (AT1e and AT1a)

All pupils should be able to select and use relevant evidence from the information on Muslim and Quaker attitudes to gambling in their dialogue. In the head and tails activity pupils should be able to match the relevant half. It would be helpful for pupils to read out their answers to help them develop their confidence in using religious terms. Correct answers would be:

a) Quakers or The Society of Friends … is a denomination of Christianity.
b) Muslims and Quakers both believe … it is wrong to take part in the lottery.

c) For Muslims gambling … is considered haram and against the will of Allah.

Further discussion could be generated concerning difficulties when religious beliefs conflict with workplace practices.

Now try this (extension work) (AT1h and AT1a) Worksheet 4.2

In the first part of the activity reference might be made to the way something could be treated as a god, for example, venerated; worshipped; a focus; sacred; particular code of living. Inclusion of religious language should be encouraged.

In the second part of the activity pupils can use their imagination to describe a relevant scenario, for example, how someone spends their time displaying how much wealth they have.

Worksheet 4.2 requires pupils to consider a range of reasons and to match relevant statements to religious and non-religious beliefs. By using colour-coding pupils will be able to see similarities and differences between religious and non-religious views.

Suggestions for homework and follow-up work

1 Use the Internet to find out more about Islamic banks.
2 Interview ten people and ask them their views on the lottery.

2 Islam teaches that it is haram to receive interest on loans as it can cause hardship to people.
3 The Qur'an states it is wrong to gamble as it is the work of Shaitan.
4 Wealth gained through the National Lottery is at the expense of others.

Humanists might not agree with any of the pictures as a way to gain wealth. Their justification would be based upon the harm that it does.

Plenary activity

All of the words and phrases are used in Lesson Two in the Pupil's Book (pages 76–79). After they have identified the words in the wordsearch, pupils should then work in pairs to give a definition of each. Phrases may appear together or as two separate words.

Suggested definitions

Five Precepts – a Buddhist moral code that is considered to be the ideal for life.
Body Shop – an organisation founded by Anita Roddick that supports social and environmental issues.
Riba – a term used in Islam for receiving interest.
Qimar – gambling.
Quakers – a Christian denomination often called Society of Friends.
National Lottery – a game of chance for which people can buy tickets to win money.

Framework RE 3 ICT Resource Teacher's Notes

Starter activity

The statements in this activity are intended to give pupils opportunities to reflect on their own attitudes to ethical trading. There is no correct order but pupils should justify their decisions.

Main activity

Through this activity pupils are applying their understanding of the teachings of three religious traditions. In their answers pupils need to justify why a religion would hold that view. By reviewing the teachings on page 34 of the Pupil's Book, pupils will be able to reinforce their previous learning.

There are four pictures in total, one on each screen. Click on the arrow at the bottom of the screen to move on to the next.

Suggested answers

1 Killing animals goes against the first of the Five Precepts (not to harm living things).

3. WHAT ABOUT THE EARTH'S RESOURCES?

Pupil's Book pages 80–83

Aim

The aim of the lesson is to teach pupils about the importance of caring for the environment.

Learning objectives

By the end of the lesson pupils should have:
- identified the results of humanity's misuse of the earth's resources (AT2d)
- suggested ways that they can learn about how to care for the earth (AT2e).

Skills involved

Pupils will be:
- identifying how humans are damaging the earth
- thinking about their own views on how we should care for the earth.

Information

Before this lesson it is important to have conducted a diagnostic assessment to ascertain pupils prior knowledge and understanding from other subject areas, such as geography. There are many opportunities for cross-curricular work through this topic.

For many people their relationship with the earth is precious. Pupils should be introduced to a range of secular and religious teachings and activities. Particular examples are the teachings of Chief Seattle who replied as follows in 1854 when an offer was made for a large area of his native American land:

'You must teach your children that the ground beneath their feet is the ashes of your grandfathers. So that they must respect the land; tell your children that the earth is rich with the lives of our kin. Teach your children what we have taught our children, that the earth is our mother. Whatever befalls the earth befalls the sons of the earth. If men spit upon the ground they spit upon themselves. This we know: the earth does not belong to man; man belongs to the earth. This we know. All things are connected like the blood which unites one family. All things are connected. Whatever befalls the earth befalls the sons of the earth. Man did not weave the web of life; he is merely a strand in it. Whatever he does to the web he does to himself. Even the white man, whose God walks and talks with him as a friend to a friend, cannot be exempt from common destiny. We may be brothers after all. We shall see. One thing we know, which the white man may one day discover our God is the same God. You may think now that you own Him as you wish to own our land;

but you cannot. He is the God of man, and his compassion is equal for the red man and the white. This earth is precious to Him, and to harm the earth is to heap contempt upon the Creator'. The Gaia Theory could also be explained.

Dr James Lovelock put forward the Gaia hypothesis. This is the theory that the earth is a living organism just as humans and animals are. It fights against the diseases which humankind inflicts upon her such as the destruction of forests and pollution of rivers. Sometimes the earth wins when it manages to grass over dumps or a quarry turns into a lake and attracts wildlife.

There are many teachings from other faith and non-faith traditions which can be investigated on websites such as www.reep.org and www.arcworld.org/faiths.htm.

Use of ICT

Research: To support Activity 1 and 2, pupils could use a range of websites such as www.reep.org and www.arcworld.org/faiths.htm.

Communication: In 'Now try this' pupils can present their work as a PowerPoint presentation.

ICT Resource: See *Framework RE 3 ICT Resource Teacher's Notes*, page 77.

Activity 1 (AT2d)

In the first part of the activity pupils have to match pictures and captions showing cause and effect. This should support the use of a range of specific terminology such as pollution; deforestation; greenhouse effect; etc.

The answers are:
a) Pollution in rivers can kill plants and wildlife (Pictures 2 and 6).
b) Deforestation destroys animal habitats and causes soil erosion (Pictures 1 and 7).
c) Not feeding animals properly can result in mad cow disease (Pictures 3 and 5).
d) Emission of gases leads to the greenhouse effect, which can cause sea levels to rise (Pictures 4 and 8).

Activity 2 (AT2d)

In this activity pupils are asked to suggest captions for the 'effect' picture. Pupils should show an understanding of the effect of an increase in population. This could include:
- overcrowding
- drain on resources
- poverty and disease
- early mortality
- increase in pollution, etc.

Activity 3 (AT2d and AT2e)

In this activity pupils are expected to engage with the points of views and to consider which they support or disagree with. This identification and justification is a developmental step for the evaluation skills needed in GCSE. Pupils could phrase their answers 'I agree that … because …'.

The range of quotes will require pupils to reflect upon their own view of God as creator of the planet.

Now try this (extension work) (AT2d)

This activity follows the theme of teaching young children about the environment. Pupils may want to consider what would be long-term or short-term education.

Suggestions for homework and follow-up work

Collect a range of visual images from the community showing misuse of the environment.

Answers
1 Greenhouse
2 Deforestation
3 Environment
4 Sustainability
5 Soil erosion
6 Pollution
7 Guardians
8 Responsibility

Example of a sentence
It is everyone's responsibility to protect the environment from pollution.

Framework RE 3 ICT Resource Teacher's Notes

Starter activity

Ask pupils in turn to identify an environmental issue. If they are able to they can remove a piece of the jigsaw. Continue until they can guess what the picture is. The picture shows a Greenpeace demonstration in Rio, Brazil, at the statue of Jesus. They were protesting about the outcome of the Earth Summit in Johannesburg in 2002 (ten years after the summit in Brazil). After the picture has been fully displayed pupils should work in pairs to develop a caption for it. Then discuss the question 'What has Jesus got to do with Greenpeace?'

Main activity

The activity gives pupils an opportunity to refer to activities that occur within their own communities. Reference could be made to:

- being responsible for their own litter
- recycling
- joining local environment organisations
- taking showers rather than baths
- running a campaign group in the school
- contacting a local politician.

Plenary activity

Pupils could be split into teams to work out the anagrams in under two minutes. The anagrams are key terms that have been used in the lesson. Some pupils/teams can then progress to the next screen, and try to use three of the terms in a sentence. Again they have two minutes to do this.

4. WHAT DO RELIGIONS SAY ABOUT CARE FOR THE ENVIRONMENT?

Pupil's Book pages 84–85

Aim

The aim of this lesson is for pupils, through independent research, to present Christian and Muslim attitudes to looking after the earth.

Learning objectives

By the end of the lesson pupils should have:
- gained knowledge and understanding of the Christian and Muslim attitude towards the care of the earth (AT1a and 1e)
- been able to express Christian and Muslim teachings about the care of the earth (AT2b and 2e)
- express their own views on how people should care for the earth.

Skills involved

Pupils will be:
- finding out about Muslim and Christian attitudes to the earth
- explaining and presenting information
- using evidence to justify their own views.

Information

In this lesson pupils are given the opportunity to work independently to produce a piece of assessed work. In addition to the previous lesson, pupils can draw on previous learning on environmental issues.

Use of ICT

Research: To find out more information about Islam and Christianity and to explore a range of relevant visual images.
Communication: Production of a Year 6 pamphlet using ICT.
ICT Resource: See *Framework RE 3 ICT Resource* Teacher's Notes (below).

Activity (AT1a, AT1e, AT2b and AT2e)

Worksheets 4.3 and 4.4

In this lesson there is one activity, which results in an assessed piece of work. Pupils should use a variety of sources and resources to complete their booklet. In the Pupil's Book there are:
- interviews
- scriptural quotes
- websites for pupils to draw from.

In addition, Worksheet 4.3 has a bank of teachings from a number of religions, which some more able pupils may want to use when making comparisons between religions.
  Some pupils will need the task broken down into smaller steps, such as in Worksheet 4.4, for example:
- group to be selected
- analysis of a range of Year 6 booklets to decide on a relevant criteria
- plan what will go into the booklet and each person's role in the group
- peer review and assessment.

Suggestions for homework and follow-up work

In groups, pupils may select five questions they would ask a Christian or Muslim visitor to the school.

Framework RE 3 ICT Resource Teacher's Notes

Main activity

This lesson has been designed as a student investigation, therefore there is only one ICT activity. This requires students to identify the assessment criteria for their booklet (see Pupil's Book, pages 84–5). It is important that pupils' responses are analysed by the teacher before they start work on their booklet so that any misconceptions can be dealt with. When they have completed their plan for their booklet they can look back at the criteria they identified as important in this activity to make sure that they have all been covered.

5. WHAT ATTITUDES DO RELIGIOUS PEOPLE HAVE TO ANIMALS?

Pupil's Book pages 86–89

Aim

The aim of this lesson is for pupils to understand the impact of beliefs on issues connected with animals.

Learning objectives

By the end of the lesson pupils should have:
- thought about different attitudes to animals (AT2d and 2e)
- analysed the impact of religious beliefs and attitudes on the welfare of animals (AT1e)
- recognised the role of interpretation of religious teachings (AT1g).

Skills involved

Pupils will be:
- identifying different attitudes that humans have towards animals
- analysing how religious beliefs can inspire actions to care for animals
- investigating a range of sources to consider whether Jesus was a vegetarian.

Use of ICT

Research: The web quest on Worksheet 4.5 requires the investigation of a range of websites.

Communication: Pupils can complete their concept map in Activity 1 and their table in Activity 2 using ICT. The results from the web quest on Worksheet 4.5 can be presented using PowerPoint.

ICT Resource: See *Framework RE 3 ICT Resource Teacher's Notes*, page 80.

Activity 1 (AT2d)

The first part of this activity is an introduction to the many different types of relationships that humankind has with animals. Some discussion may ensue concerning the different power roles, for example, rider to horse/hunter to fox/guide dog to owner.

In the second part of the activity there is no one answer. Animal liberationists would say all lives are the same. Questions may be developed concerning whether it matters how many dogs there are – or is the distinction because it is an animal?

Activity 2 (AT1g, AT1e and AT2d)
Worksheet 4.5

Pupils are asked to read the information concerning the religious teachings and the animal care projects. In the activity pupils are expected to be able to link and explain the effect of the religious belief or teaching upon the nature of the project.

Answers could include the following points:

Buddhism

What are they doing?
- Running a sanctuary for tigers.

Why is there a need?
- Poachers are killing many tigers.

What are the religious principles?
- The *Ahchoranga Sutra* states the importance of treating all creatures well.
- A belief in reincarnation means the tigers may have been past friends.
- (Reference may be made to the Five Precepts.)

Hinduism

What are they doing?
- Protecting cows in India and in Hindu communities across the world.

Why is there a need?
- Mistreatment of cows.
- Cows are revered by Hindus and should be given respect.

What are the religious principles?
- In Hinduism the cow has a special status and is revered.
- Belief in ahimsa.
- Example of Krishna who was a cow-herder.
- The Bhagavad Gita states that by serving animals people can attain happiness.

Islam

What are they doing?
- The IFEES Project in Tanzania protects the turtle nesting sites.

Why is there a need?
- The sites were in danger from dynamite fishing.

What are the religious principles?
- The Qur'an states how important it is not to waste.
- Animals should only be killed for a useful purpose.

The information gained from the first part of the activity will feed into the web quest activity on Worksheet 4:5. A web quest has five basic elements:

1 Introduction
2 Task
3 Process
4 Evaluation
5 Conclusion.

There is helpful information available on www.webquest.org.

The worksheet allows pupils to continue to investigate faith-based projects to produce a PowerPoint presentation. Teachers may direct pupils to investigate particular religions depending upon which are going to be studied at Key Stage 4.

Activity 3 (AT1g and AT2e)

The first part of the activity requires pupils to assess a range of statements and to make an informed and justified opinion.

In the second part of the activity pupils will need to consider the role of Jesus' teachings and practices for Christians. Answers may include:

● To be a true Christian means you should follow all the practices of Jesus.
● Christians believe they were given free will so it's up to them and their conscience.

Now try this (extension work) (AT2e)

This activity requires pupils to engage with and be able to explain the quote. For some pupils it may be supportive to give them a bank of key words to use in their descriptions, for example, stewards, creation, humanity.

They should then label the different groups, giving a heading to their classification and reasons for their choices. The four obvious classifications are food, sport, work and companionship but pupils may come up with others such as a support in life, as a need, as a want, for entertainment, to abuse.

Main activity

This activity is designed to get pupils thinking about where they stand on issues concerning animals. They need to realise there is a difference of opinion on many of the topics and that certain circumstances will often make a difference, for example the purposes for which animals are used in experiments.

There are six statements in total, one on each screen. Click on the arrow at the bottom of the screen to move on to the next.

Plenary activity

This activity consolidates the learning across the lesson. Pupils are asked to drag and drop the correct words into the sentences. You could ask them to define each word as it is inserted into place. There are two screens in total. Click on the arrow at the bottom of the screen to go on to the next.

Answers

1 sacred texts
2 reincarnation, sacred
3 Hindus
4 ahimsa
5 Day of Judgement
6 God's creation

Framework RE 3 ICT Resource Teacher's Notes

Starter activity

Pupils should drag and drop the different examples of humans' relationships with animals to make four different groups.

The examples are:
Steak
Guide dog
Fox hunting
Riding a horse
Sniffer dog
Pet
Mountain Rescue Dog
Zoos
Medical experiments

6. WHAT MAKES US STRONG?

Pupil's Book pages 90–93

Aim

The aim of this lesson is to learn about how people develop their inner resources and identify opportunities for spiritual development.

Learning objectives

By the end of the lesson pupils should have:
- gained an understanding of the importance of spiritual qualities (AT1h)
- been able to identify what spiritual qualities are (AT1f)
- developed an awareness of the different ways people can develop their well-being (AT2c)
- reflected upon their own spiritual qualities (AT1e and 2e).

Skills involved

Pupils will be:
- identifying spiritual qualities
- thinking about their own spiritual qualities
- finding out how people look after their inner strength
- using their imagination to think about how their school can develop spiritual qualities.

Information

The life of Nkosi Johnson can be found on www.myhero.com. He was one of the 70,000 children born HIV-positive in South Africa. His mother became too weak to look after him and he became a foster child of a volunteer worker Gail Johnson. Together they began a life of many battles such as trying to get him into a school. In July 2000 at the age of 11 he made a public speech at an International Aids conference. He was probably the longest surviving child in South Africa with aids.

Use of ICT

Research: Various websites which specialise in spiritual development through music, art and the environment, for example, www.heavenlyspaces.co.uk and www.pcfre.org.uk/spiritedarts. Further information concerning apartheid for the first activity can be found at www.teachersparadise.com and www.cafod.org.uk.

Communication: The diagram in Activity 1 could be produced using ICT, as could the plan in the 'Now try this' activity.

ICT Resource: See *Framework RE 3 ICT Resource Teacher's Notes*, page 82.

Activity 1 (AT1h and AT1f) Worksheet 4.6

The song has been used for an anthem for many human rights issues, for example, apartheid in South Africa. This could be explained as follows:

The Apartheid system was introduced into South Africa in the 1950s. It meant that people were separated or segregated according to the colour of their skins. This resulted in separate living areas, schools, buses and even entrances to public services. Many people such as Steve Biko, Trevor Huddleston, Bishop Tutu and Nelson Mandela actively campaigned to bring the system to an end.

In the second part of the activity, pupils should have a wide selection of people to choose from. You could prompt them with suggestions such as people discriminated against because of their religion/sex/age/disability or sexuality. Pupils could look through a range of newspapers for topical examples. It is important that their justification reflects their understanding of someone who has succeeded in the face of adversity or oppression.

In the third part of the activity pupils reflect upon their own spiritual qualities. Prior to the task it is important to check that pupils have a working knowledge of the terms. The worksheet will support pupils to identify the qualities.

Activity 2 (AT2c)

In this activity pupils read and analyse a range of different quotes about well-being.

Suggestions for Joe and Helen could include laughing; communication with others; love; voluntary work; following a religion.

Activity 3 (AT2c and AT2e)

Through the life story of Nkosi Johnson, pupils will able to reflect upon the spiritual qualities shown and to express their own beliefs and ideas. There are no set answers for the two parts of this activity. Higher ability pupils could gain more information on Nkosi on www.myhero.com and rank order his inner strengths, giving a brief justification with relevant examples.

Now try this (extension work) (AT1e and AT2e)

This can be a structured exercise where pupils are put into groups to consider parts of school life, for example, lunch-times; playground; corridors; assemblies; etc. and then for a whole school plan to be devised. This can be produced using ICT. There may be opportunities for pupils to present their findings to a school council.

Suggestions for homework and follow-up work Worksheet 4.7

Pupils could investigate the inner qualities of people who have shown courage in times of adversity. Pupils may identify other people they know in the community or throughout the world.

Framework RE 3 ICT Resource Teacher's Notes

Starter activity

After eleven years of study Professor Michael Argyle has analysed thousands of questionnaires and come up with an answer to what makes people happy. Pupils should decide what things, according to Professor Argyle, make people happy. The activity could then be extended to see whether they agree with his conclusions. Some pupils could then be asked to consider whether each answer would produce short- or long-term happiness.

There are eleven statements in total, split over two screens. Click on the arrow at the bottom of the screen to move on to the next.

Answers

1 Going out on shopping sprees (False)

2 Watching TV soaps with friends and family (True)

3 Marriage (True)

4 Playing a sport with other people (True)

5 A hobby that challenges you (True)

6 Working hard at something (True)

7 Extra-marital affairs (False)

8 Attending a place of worship (True)

9 Brisk fifteen-minute walk (True)

10 Having close friends (True)

11 Money (False) (only the very poor are happier)

Main activity

Pupils should categorise each of the opportunities for spiritual development into those that are religious, secular or both. The subjects are:

Candles

Good food

Music

Prayer

Retreats

Sharing an activity with the community

Silence

Reading.

Through completing the activity pupils should be aware that spiritual development is not dependent upon someone belonging to an organised religious tradition. The activity should support the Now Try This activity on page 93 of the Pupil's Book.

Suggested answers

Religious: Prayer

Secular: Good food

Both: Candles, Music, Retreats, Sharing an activity with the community, Silence, Reading

Plenary activity

This activity allows students to reflect on the key issues of the lesson. Although there are no right or wrong answers, students should be able to justify their stance.

There are five statements in total, one on each screen. Click on the arrow at the bottom of the screen to move on to the next.

FRAMEWORK RE 3

Worksheet 4.1

Use this worksheet to help you with Activity One.

Task

Cut out or use a highlighter to sort the quotes into the following categories:
1. You can't take it with you when you go.
2. Wealth is maya – it is an illusion that doesn't last.
3. The real measure of our wealth is how much we would be worth if we lost all our money.

Buddhism

'Of all gains, good health is the greatest,

Of all wealth, contentment is the greatest.'

Dhammapada 203:5

'Whoever in your kingdom is poor, to him let some help be given.'

Cakkatti Sidhananda Sutta

Christianity

'Watch out! Be on your guard against all kinds of greed; a man's life does not consist in the abundance of his possessions.'

Luke 12:15

'"Good teacher," he asked, "What must I do to inherit eternal life?" ... and Jesus said, "Go, sell everything you have and give to the poor and you will have treasure in heaven."'

Mark 10 17:21

'You cannot serve both God and money.'

Matthew 6:24

'The love of money causes all kinds of evil.'

1 Timothy 6:10

Hinduism

'The riches of those who are generous never waste away, while those who will not give find none to comfort them.'

Rig Veda 10:117

'The desire for wealth can never bring happiness.'

Mahabharata Shavi Parva

FRAMEWORK RE 3

Worksheet 4.1 (continued)

Islam

'A man who helps and spends his time and money looking after widows and the poor holds the same position in the eyes of God as one who fights in a war, or fasts every day and prays the whole night for a number of years.'
Hadith

'Richness does not lie in abundance of worldly goods, but true richness is the richness of the soul.'
Hadith

Judaism

'Cast but a glance at riches, and they are gone, for they will surely sprout wings and fly off to the sky like an eagle.'
Proverbs 23:5

'Who is rich? He who is satisfied with what he has.'
Ethics of the Fathers

Sikhism

'Wealth, youth and flowers are short-lived as guests for four short days.
Be grateful to God whose bounties you enjoy. Be compassionate to the needy and the people you employ.'
Guru Granth Sahib 23

FRAMEWORK RE 3

Worksheet 4.2

Use this worksheet to help you with the 'Now try this' activity.

Information

Ahmad is an eighteen-year-old Muslim who is studying Computer Science at University.

Helen is a seventeen-year-old Quaker who is part of a girl band called Faith.

Leroy does not believe in God. He is nineteen years old and works for a charity which helps people in poverty in Britain.

Ahmad, Helen and Leroy all refuse to take part in the lottery or any form of gambling.

Tasks

1. Choose four different colour pens or pencils.

2. Use one colour to highlight reasons why Ahmad doesn't support the lottery, another for why Helen doesn't support the lottery, and a third for why Leroy doesn't support the lottery.

3. Use a different colour to colour in the boxes that could apply to all.

4. Leave blank the boxes that you think have no relevancy.

Ahmad practices Islam and has done so all his life.	Ahmad's mother is Muslim and father is Hindu.	Ahmad and Leroy work in the same office.
Many people have become homeless through gambling.	People win the lottery at the expense of others.	Leroy, Ahmad and Helen went on the march protesting against the war.
The Qur'an says that games of chance are the work of Shaitan.	Some people say the lottery goes against the Christian ethos.	The lottery is held twice a week.
Winning the lottery doesn't mean you'll be happy.	Ahmad doesn't get on with the person who collects the lottery money.	Many people go into debt because of gambling.
The lottery helps many local and national causes.	Some people don't agree with some of the causes that the lottery money is spent on.	People who win money in the lottery do so at the expense of others.
The lottery has made many people millionaires.	Many of the causes that the lottery supports are not religious.	

FRAMEWORK RE 3

Worksheet 4.3

Use this worksheet to help you with your booklet for Year 6.

Religious Teachings

Judaism

Jews believe they have a duty to look after the world which God has created and has been loaned to them:

'Teachers must see that children respect the smallest and largest animals which, like people, have feelings. The children who get enjoyment from the convulsions of an injured beetle will grow up to be insensitive to suffering.'
Rabbi SR Hirsch

Hinduism

As Hindus believe all living beings have atman (self or soul) so they consider all life to be precious:

'For every hair on the body of a beast, the person who kills it without reason will be slaughtered in successive births.'
Manu 5:38

Islam

'Eat and drink: but waste not by excess for Allah loveth not the wasters.'

Buddhism

'All breathing, existing living sentient creatures should not be slain or treated with violence, nor abused, nor tormented, nor driven away.'
Anchoranga Sutra

'According to Buddhism the life of all beings – human, animal or otherwise – is precious and we all have the same right to happiness.'
The Dalai Lama Beyond Dogma

Humanists

For most humanists the reason to care for the world would be connected with human happiness and welfare which is dependent on the environment and the existence of many species.

FRAMEWORK RE 3

Worksheet 4.4

Use this worksheet to help you with your booklet for Year 6.

Objective

I have to produce a booklet to explain the _____ attitude to the earth which could be used with a Year 6 class. Before I begin my research I need to look at the assessment criteria and see what is needed for each level.

To reach level 4 I will need to use some religious vocabulary to describe the attitude to the environment. I will be able to suggest what is meant by any quotes I use. I will have chosen an appropriate illustration and be able to state why.

To reach level 5 I will need to use a wide range of religious vocabulary to explain the attitude to the environment. I will describe in my own words what is meant by any quotes I use and how they relate to beliefs in each religion. I will give a justification of my choice of illustration.

To reach level 6 I will need to use a wide range of religious vocabulary to give a detailed explanation. I will show how the attitude has an impact on the life of the believer. I will explain in my own words what believers understand by the quotes I use. I will give a detailed justification of my choice of illustration linking my explanation to the main beliefs of the religions.

First step

The main content I am going to include is …

* _____
  _____

* _____
  _____

* _____
  _____

* _____
  _____

FRAMEWORK RE 3

Worksheet 4.4 (continued)

Second step

The quote that I think is most important for each religion ...
Christianity _____

Islam _____

I think this means ...
Christianity _____
Islam _____

Third step

I have used an Internet site and found out more information I want to include ...

- _____
- _____
- _____

Fourth step

The three questions I would ask a Christian or Muslim are ...

_____

_____

_____

Their answers should give me information about ...

_____

_____

_____

Fifth step

I have decided to use a picture of _____ for the front page of my booklet because

_____

Sixth step

I will look again at the assessment criteria which I have been given and indicate the level I think I have achieved.

- Level _____

FRAMEWORK RE 3

Worksheet 4.5

Use this worksheet to help you with Activity Two.

WEB QUEST: 'Religions do little to care for animals'

Task

You will need to investigate a faith-based project to respond to the statement above.

To do this you will need to prepare a PowerPoint presentation.

The Process

1.   Choose a project. Some are suggested below with their websites, or you could choose another.

- www.noahproject.org.uk
- www.khalsaenvironmentproject.org
- www.arcworld.org
- www.christianveg.com
- www.tigertemple.org/Eng/index.htm
- www.ruralministry.com
- www.ifees.org.uk/

2.   Plan ways that you could make your presentation interesting and make your audience think about the issues, such as using relevant pictures, including quotes to reflect upon, etc.

3.   Explain the work of the project using pictures.

4.   Show how the work and action of the project links with the religious teachings and beliefs.

5.   Select another project and prepare a final slide to show the main similarities and differences between the two.

FRAMEWORK RE 3

Worksheet 4.6

Use this worksheet to help you with Activity One.

Task

The Word Bank below contains a list of your inner strengths. Place each in the circle according to how you value them in your life.

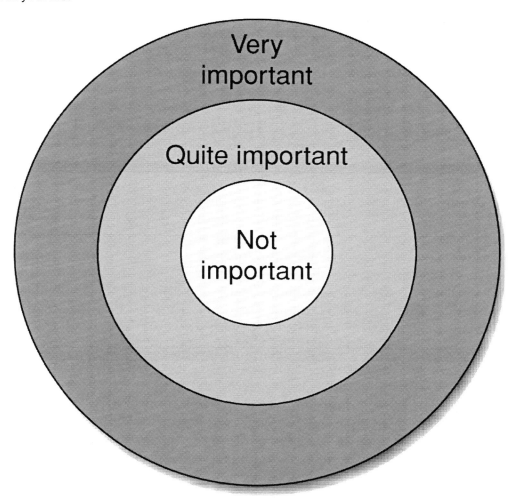

Very important

Quite important

Not important

Word Bank

- self-control
- patience
- humility
- gratitude
- peace

- love
- gentleness
- faith
- hope
- forgiveness

- humanity
- courage
- perseverance
- goodness
- truth

- beauty
- justice
- freedom

FRAMEWORK RE 3

Worksheet 4.7

Use this worksheet to help you with your homework.

Tasks

1. Read the information and quote about John McCarthy.
2. Use the Word Bank below to complete the diamond with the qualities you think John McCarthy had to show when he was held hostage.

John McCarthy was a 29-year-old British journalist who, on his first foreign assignment, was captured driving to Beirut airport to get his plane home to London. He was blindfolded and stripped of his belongings and not rescued for five years.

'I am still and always will be amazed at the qualities men find in themselves when they have only themselves in which to find a source of life. I had seen John McCarthy turn from someone who was frightened … into someone who was unafraid and totally committed to life.'
From *An Evil Cradling* by Brian Keenan

Word Bank

- self-control
- patience
- humility
- gratitude
- peace
- love
- gentleness
- faith
- hope
- forgiveness
- humanity
- courage
- perseverance
- goodness
- truth
- beauty
- justice
- freedom
- inner strength

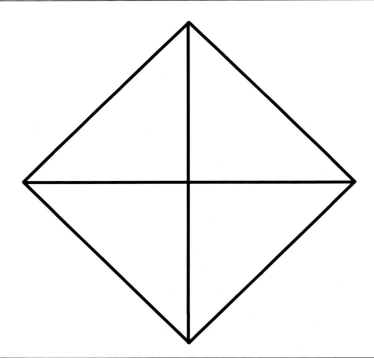

UNIT 5: HOW DO BELIEFS AFFECT PEACE AND CONFLICT IN THE WORLD TODAY?

Introduction

The purpose of this unit is to explore many different aspects of conflict and peace. Throughout this unit pupils will be considering a range of different case studies and reflecting upon the implications of a range of religious and non-religious beliefs.

Contents

The unit begins by looking at the impact of a range of religious attitudes to conflict. This is built upon in the second lesson when a diversity of views are considered within one religious tradition. In the third lesson pupils learn about and reflect upon a range of different initiatives to make and keep peace and this is further developed in the fourth lesson when specific case studies are investigated concerning the impact of inter-faith dialogue and action. The fifth lesson considers the role of forgiveness in reconciliation and long-term peace-keeping. The unit concludes with a consideration of when conflict may be necessary to establish human rights. There are opportunities for pupils to reflect upon a range of relevant case studies, and to utilise their learning from previous lessons through case studies which look at when it may be necessary to challenge peace because of beliefs.

Appendices

- Appendix A: Record of achievement chart.
- Appendix B: Grid identifying the various learning styles, skills and methods employed in each lesson.

APPENDIX A

FRAMEWORK RE 3: RECORD OF ACHIEVEMENT
UNIT 5

PUPIL NAME: _____   GROUP: _____   TEACHER: _____

LESSON	AT1 Activity	AT1 Mark	AT2 Activity	AT2 Mark
1	1			
			2	
			3	
	4		4	
	NTT			
2	1			
	2			
	3			
	NTT			
3	1		1	
			2	
			NTT	
4			1	
			2	
	3		3	
			4	
	NTT		NTT	
5			1	
	2		2	
	3			
	NTT			
6			1	
	2			
	3		3	
	NTT		NTT	
LEVEL				

NOTES ON PROGRESS:

TARGETS:

Signed (Pupil) _____   Signed (Teacher) _____

APPENDIX B

UNIT 5: COVERAGE OF LEARNING ACTIVITIES, STYLES, METHODS, SKILLS

	Lesson 1	Lesson 2	Lesson 3	Lesson 4	Lesson 5	Lesson 6
Classification	✖					
Most likely						
Odd one out					✖	
Reveal			✖		✖	✖
Sequencing						
Show me						
Reflective questioning	✖	✖	✖	✖		✖
Multiple choice					✖	
Ranking					✖	
Drag and drop						
Matching				✖		
Filling in gaps						
Writing	✖	✖	✖	✖	✖	✖
Brainstorming	✖	✖		✖	✖	✖
Discussion	✖	✖	✖	✖	✖	✖
Comparing	✖			✖		✖
Investigating		✖		✖		✖
Questioning	✖	✖	✖	✖	✖	
Explaining	✖	✖	✖	✖	✖	✖
Giving accounts	✖					✖
Mind map					✖	
Evaluating					✖	
Imagining		✖		✖		✖
Analysing			✖		✖	✖
Synthesising				✖		
Empathising	✖	✖	✖	✖		✖
Criticising						
Negotiating	✖	✖		✖	✖	
Deciding	✖	✖	✖	✖	✖	✖
Expressing clearly	✖	✖	✖	✖	✖	✖
Listening	✖	✖	✖	✖	✖	✖
Interpreting	✖	✖				✖
Applying	✖	✖				✖
Responding	✖	✖	✖	✖	✖	✖
Observing	✖	✖	✖			
Learning styles						
Kinaesthetic						
Auditory			✖			
Visual			✖	✖	✖	✖

1. WHY ARE THERE CONFLICTS?

Pupil's Book, pages 96–99

Aim

The aim of this lesson is to teach pupils that there are a range of religious and non-religious views concerning issues of war and conflict.

Learning objectives

By the end of the lesson pupils should have:
- interpreted teachings from religions about conflict and war (AT1a and 1e)
- been able to define the key terms: just war, conscientious objector, holy war and pacifism (AT1f)
- identified different types of conflict (AT2d)
- reflected on and discussed what makes a war 'just' (AT2d).

Skills involved

Pupils will be:
- identifying different types of conflict.
- interpreting teachings from religions about conflict and war
- thinking about what makes a war 'just'.

Information

Within each religious tradition there are a range of different views concerning conflict and taking part in wars. An example of this is within the Buddhist tradition. Pupils will often raise the issue of martial arts.

The Shaolin monks forbid the monk from ever being the aggressor and they are only allowed to use a limited amount of force. Most martial arts traditions have strong spiritual elements and insist on as little violence as possible being used.

Of the major world religions it is only the Jains which have not been involved in warfare.

Use of ICT

ICT Resource: See *Framework RE 3 ICT Resource* Teacher's Notes, page 97.

Activity 1 (AT2d)

This activity should help pupils make connections with past learning. It requires pupils to engage with the book and to investigate a range of pictures, thereby developing visual literacy.

Examples may include:
- examples of discrimination (Unit 1)
- apartheid in South Africa (Unit 5)
- the church in China (Unit 1)
- the environment (Unit 4)
- the Civil Rights Movement in the USA (Rosa Parks, Martin Luther King, etc) (Unit 1, 5).

Depending upon the class situation pupils could also have a range of papers and magazines and have five minutes to find any examples of conflict.

Activity 2 (AT2d)

Pupils should be given a time limit to study the picture before discussing the contents. The soldier is an Orthodox Jew who is about to pray whilst carrying a gun. The three clues that he is about to pray are:
- Teffilah shel rosh – This is part of the tefillin. It is a box bound to the head with a strap. The box contains the first two paragraphs of the shema. It reminds the wearer that he must serve God with his mind, for example by developing thoughts of justice towards people.
- Tallith or prayer shawl.
- Siddur or prayer book.

For the third part of the activity pupils may refer to the incongruity of prayer and worship and weapons of war. Titles may refer to this incongruity such as 'Is this what God wants?', 'Why?', 'Are his prayers answered?'

Activity 3 (AT1f and AT2d) Worksheet 5.1

Worksheet 5.1 consolidates pupils understanding of the conditions of a just war and is a good recap of learning before pupils complete Activity 3. The conditions *not* applicable to a just war would be:
- A country doesn't like the fact there is more oil in another country.
- A person says three times 'let's have a war'.
- Hospitals and schools are the first targets to be bombed.
- People vote to go to war.
- To defend your religion.

Activity 3 requires pupils to develop an understanding of the concept of just war and to make further justifications. This activity leads them to analyse the relevance of the just war theory today. The task is open-ended and pupils should be assessed by the quality of their reasoning.

Activity 4 (AT1a and AT1f)

In this activity pupils will read through the teachings of a range of religious and non-religious traditions before completing an information table. It should be made explicit that individuals of any faith or non-faith group may be conscientious objectors.

Now try this (extension work) (AT1a and AT1e)

In this extension activity pupils need to show an understanding of the moral conflict indicated by St Cyprian's comment. Examples may include:

- taking of land
- taking of property
- forcing people to fight
- people captured and detained
- censorship.

Suggestions for homework and follow-up work

1 Investigate one religion's views on war that you have not studied so far .Use the Internet and other resources available.
2 Write a poem expressing your views about war.
3 Find pictures of different types of conflict to put on the class display.

Framework RE 3 ICT Resource Teacher's Notes

Starter activity

Pupils are asked to look at different types of violence and, for each type, to decide whether it is always acceptable, sometimes acceptable or never acceptable. Pupils should be aware that the answers are subjective and so there are no right or wrong answers. What is important is how pupils can justify each of their responses.

Main activity

Pupils are asked to define some of the words that they have covered in Lesson One in Pupil's Book pages 96–99. The activity can be used to consolidate the meaning of a number of words that can be used in a GCSE answer of peace and conflict. You could extend this activity and ask pupils to apply their understanding by using four of these words in a paragraph describing attitudes to war.

Suggested answers

1 Just War – A theory that outlines the conditions necessary for it to be right to go to war.
2 Jihad – Every Muslim's individual struggle to resist evil in order to follow the path of Allah; also used to describe collective defence.
3 Conscience – A person's sense of what is right and wrong
4 Stereotype – A person or thing considered to represent a group.
5 Pacifism – Belief that all war is wrong.
6 Holy War – War fought in defence of religion or religious teachings.

Plenary activity

Pupils will be able to consolidate their learning in Lesson One in the Pupil's Book (pages 96–99) by deciding whether statements about different religious attitudes to war are true or false. Some of the answers revisit Unit One, Lesson Five, which showed the importance of not using stereotypes when referring to believers of a faith tradition. After they have answered, pupils should attempt to correct the false statements.

Answers

1 The greater jihad in Islam is when you take part in a war. False. The greater jihad is the struggle within oneself. Taking part in a war is the lesser jihad.
2 All Buddhists are pacifists. False. Some Buddhists are pacifists.
3 A just war has certain rules. True.
4 The Crusades are an example of a Holy War. True.
5 Humanists do not agree with war. False. Some Humanists do not agree with war.

2. WHY ARE THERE DIFFERENT CHRISTIAN ATTITUDES TO WAR?

Pupil's Book pages 100–103

Aim

The aim of this lesson is to teach pupils the different attitudes of Christian denominations concerning war.

Learning objectives

By the end of the lesson pupils should have:
- gained a knowledge and understanding of different denominations' attitudes to war (AT1a)
- compared different denominations' attitudes to war (AT1c and 1h)
- investigated what the Bible says about wars (AT1b and 1g).

Skills involved

Pupils will be:
- thinking about whether Christians should take part in wars
- investigating what the Bible says about wars
- comparing beliefs and practices of different denominations.

Information

This lesson explores a range of Christian denominations, some of which, (for example, Jehovah Witnesses) are usually considered as a member of the broader Christian Church. Through the study of one issue, pupils will understand that there are many different views within Christianity on different social issues.

Jehovah Witnesses will not usually take part in wars and many were persecuted during the Holocaust for being conscientious objectors. They do not recognise national allegiances and so will not normally sing the National Anthem or take part in any nationalistic activity.

Use of ICT

Research: To use the Internet to find further information on the different denominations. www.paxchristi.org.uk will give further information for Activity 3.

Communication: Pupils could word process their answer to Activity 3, part 2, therefore allowing redrafting. Activity 2, part 3 could be presented using ICT – pupils could scan in the template on Worksheet 5.2. Activity 2, part 4 could also be presented using ICT. The homework activity requires pupils to present their findings in the form of a PowerPoint slide.

ICT Resource: See *Framework RE 3 ICT Resource Teacher's Notes*, page 99.

Information

The helmet in the picture on page 100 of the Pupil's Book contains part of Pslam 23.

There are many different versions of this Psalm.

Activity 1 (AT1a)

In the first part of this activity pupils need to study the two pictures and decide which attitudes towards war each shows. In picture 1 reference may be made to the whole of Psalm 23 and why a soldier might have written it on his or her helmet before going into battle.

In the second part of the activity pupils are required to suggest influences on decision-making. The activity asks pupils to reflect on the considerations that a Christian might make. Pupils should be made to justify their choices. Some pupils may consider what happens if two influences conflict (for example, what friends and family think and what the Bible teaches).

In the third part of the activity pupils may draw on previous learning on beliefs, practices and traditions within Christianity. During this activity the teacher may give some supporting words, which would focus pupils' attention on different parts of their previous learning, for example, baptism; mass; priests; crucifix; the Pope.

Activity 2 (AT1a and AT1c) Worksheet 5.2

The first part of this activity requires pupils to consider the different ways that they may research a topic, for example, the Internet; ask a person from that faith; use a textbook; send an e-mail to a believer; etc.

The second part of this activity is an example of spiral learning where pupils are expected to employ their familiarity with previous subject material they have learned about in Unit 2 Lesson 5.

In the third part of the activity, the use of a tree is a common way to express the concept of denominations. Worksheet 5.2 provides a template of this tree. Through this activity pupils are distinguishing between distinctive beliefs and practices. Examples of denominations that *would* fight include Baptists, Church of England and Methodist. Examples of religions that *would not* fight include Jehovah Witnesses, Mennonites and Religious Society of Friends (Quakers).

In the final part of the activity, the use of a Venn diagram allows pupils to express their knowledge and understanding of differences and similarities. Teachers may wish to select denominations which will be revisited in Key Stage 4.

Activity 3 (AT1b and AT1g) Worksheet 5.3

In the first part of this activity pupils will need to sort the quotes. Some pupils may decide that certain quotes aren't relevant, as they do not refer to war and the taking of other's lives. Pupils should use the evidence they collect to write the answer to the question: 'Does the Bible teach that people should go to war?' For some pupils a semi-structure may help them, for example:

I think the Bible teaches that ……………. because ………………………………….

One particular example is …………………………………

However some would say that there is a different view because ……………………...………………………………

…………. ………………………………………………

Limiting the word-count to 50 words means that pupils can redraft their answer more easily. This could take the form of peer assessment where the partner identifies ways to refine the answer.

Worksheet 5.3 extends this activity so that pupils have to analyse the different sources in the Pupil's Book that Christians would refer to before making their decisions in answer to a relevant key question. An example of a question is given but other questions may include:

- What does the Bible teach?
- Is it a just war?
- What does my denomination teach?

Now try this (extension work) (AT1h)

This extension task requires pupils to have understood the concept of 'just war' and to be able to respond to the statement.

Suggestions for homework and follow-up work

In pairs pupils present five main points about a denomination in the form of a PowerPoint slide. Each presentation should contain some historical data, some geographical data, distinctive beliefs, practices and traditions. The slides could be amalgamated to provide a resource which could be used during the course when pupils need to explore different denominational practices.

Framework RE 3 ICT Resource Teacher's Notes

Starter activity

Students are often confused about denominations of Christianity. The Pupil's Book has already introduced students to all the examples given.

Answers
Church of England
Baptist
Roman Catholic
Quakers
Methodists

Main activity

Through this activity students identify a central teaching from a number of Christian traditions. It may be appropriate for some pupils to use the Pupil's Book (page 101) for reference.

Answers

1 Church of England. We have never condemned war and live according to the Just War.

2 Jehovah Witness. We are conscientious objectors. In the Second World War many of our religion were put into concentration camps because they refused to fight.

3 Methodist. Weapons of mass destruction should never be used.

4 Quaker. Our peace testimony states that we deny all wars.

5 Roman Catholic. We consider the only reason to use nuclear weapons is to prevent wars. We would listen to the Pope's teachings as a source of authority.

Plenary activity

The plenary will identify the key teaching points from the lesson. Many new terms will have been introduced in the lesson so the key words will help clarification. The choice of key words supports differentiation.

3. HOW CAN PEACE BE MADE AND KEPT?

Pupil's Book pages 104–107

Aim
The aim of this lesson is to teach pupils about the different ways that peace can be made and kept.

Learning objectives
By the end of the lesson pupils should have:
- distinguished between making and keeping the peace (AT1h and 2e)
- analysed effective strategies of creating peace (AT2d)
- reflected upon ways of keeping peace in the local community (AT2d).

Skills involved
Pupils will be:
- recognising the difference between keeping and making peace
- finding out about two peace-keeping organisations
- comparing and deciding about strategies for keeping the peace
- thinking about the importance of peace memorials.

Information
The focus of the lesson is the way that peace is created and kept. There are many different examples. Each has its own website and could be explored for further research.

There may be opportunities to investigate and compare the work of United Nations and Pax Christi.

United Nations began in 1945 and is a secular organisation in which 51 nations are committed to working together for international peace, security and co-operation. It has many different activities such as sending peace-keeping forces to places of conflict and actively working on peace-keeping projects in countries throughout the world.

Pax Christi is an international Christian peacemaking movement, which is based on the Christian gospel and aims to create a world where people can live in peace. They work to create peace in local communities and between nations. They hold Peace Sunday Churches in church and educate young people in peaceful ways of resolving conflict.

After the US atomic bombing of her home in Hiroshima, Japan, Sadako contracted leukaemia. She promised to fold 1000 paper cranes saying:

'Paper crane I will write peace on your wings and you will fly all over the world'.

She only managed 644 before she died at the age of 12. After her death the community worked together to complete the rest and the paper crane has become a symbol of world peace. To remember her life a statue of Sadako holding a golden crane in her hand has been placed in the Hiroshima Peace Park. The writing on the base says:

'This is our cry, this is our prayer; peace in the world'.

In 2004, 120 million paper cranes were dropped over an area in southern Thailand where 540 people had died in violent clashes.

References may be made to other individuals who have dedicated their lives to creating and keeping the peace. Bertrand Russell was imprisoned for being a conscientious objector during the First World War. In 1958 he became president of the Campaign for Nuclear Disarmament. He led many campaigns of civil disobedience in protest at Britain's atomic weapons including demonstrations and mass sit-ins.

Use of ICT
Research: Use websites such as www.paxchristi.org.uk and www.peacenow-uk.org to investigate each of the projects in Activity 2.

Communication: In Activity 2 pupils could present their project justification using PowerPoint.

ICT Resource: See *Framework RE 3 ICT Resource Teacher's Notes*, page 101.

Activity 1 (AT1h and AT2e)   Worksheet 5.4
In the first part of this activity pupils have to analyse how one example of conflict can spiral to include many more people. Pupils should recognise that the conflict began with one person and ended with many more. Pupils may be able to reflect on similar situations in their own lives although they shouldn't be forced or expected to discuss these within the class unless they volunteer.

Pupils should define the difference between making and keeping the peace. Some pupils may also consider the term 'creating peace'. Through this activity pupils may consider which comes first – making/creating or keeping the peace. There should be mention of the importance of keeping the peace so that conflicts don't occur. References to the work of United Nations and Pax Christi may be relevant.

Worksheet 5.4 is used in Activities 1 and 2. In this activity pupils should read the quotes and highlight those they agree with.

Activity 2 (AT2d)   Worksheets 5.4. and 5.5
Through this activity pupils are introduced to a wide range of peace-keeping activities. After consideration they should analyse the data against the criteria and reach a justified evaluation. Pupils must have focused on the criteria before

they begin their work. The teacher may provide pupils with some examples to discuss. To give developed justifications, pupils may do further research using relevant websites especially www.peacenow.org.uk. Some candidates may be supported if they are provided with the considerations below to help their justifications:

Project one – Music
- Members of the community working together.
- Recordings could be made which could be sent to other people.
- Only musical people could be involved.

Project Two – Peace sit-ins
- Only a small number of people would be involved.
- A form of non-violent protest.
- How would they explain their protest if they were silent?
- People would be curious.

Project Three – Peace art
- Where would these paintings be placed?
- They would show the community working together.
- They would be a reminder for a long time.
- All ages would be involved.
- Who would pay?

Project Four – Paper birds of peace
- All members of the community could be involved.
- Where would they be placed?
- Messages could be written on the wings.

On Worksheet 5.5 pupils need to give their reasons for the quote they have chosen from Worksheet 5.4 for their project.

Now try this (extension work) (AT2d)
Pupils could begin this activity by thinking about the war memorials they know and considering what their role is. To support evaluation skills, some pupils should be able to give a justified reason for and against the statement.

Suggestions for homework and follow-up work
Investigate peace-keeping activities in your local community.

Framework RE 3 ICT Resource Teacher's Notes

Starter activity
Pupils have two minutes to suggest a number of different organisations and to arrange them into local, national and international groups. Examples could include:
- interfaith organisations
- marches
- joining organisations like Pax Christi
- United Nations going on peace-keeping activities, etc.

Main activity
This activity asks students to rearrange a series of sentences to respond to the statement 'Peace is a group effort.' This will help students to understand how a good answer may be constructed and they should start to become aware of the structure of answers that are needed for GCSE.

There is no right or wrong answer, although pupils should ensure they have structured the answer to give different points of view. Pupils may compare their answers and produce a peer assessment.

Plenary activity
This provides an opportunity for pupils to be still and reflect on the meaning of the poem *Reminder* by Benjamin Zephaniah. Pupils may need to be reminded of the behaviour expected before the reflection takes place and for all writing equipment to be cleared from the tables. After reading the poem pupils should explain to their partners what they think the poem means.

Suggested answers
- We spend more time thinking about war memorials than considering the importance of celebrating peace.
- Peace is often seen as coming after war, but peace was first and then came war.
- Many people think it is important to have war memorials to remember the people who have died in wars.

4. HOW CAN RELIGIONS WORK TOGETHER TO CREATE PEACE?

Pupil's Book pages 108–111

Aim
The aim of this lesson is to show how religious groups are working together to promote local, national and international harmony.

Learning objectives
By the end of the lesson pupils should have:
- been able to suggest ways of achieving religious harmony (AT2d)
- gained knowledge and understanding of projects to promote harmony between religions (AT1a and 2b)
- expressed views on their own interfaith project (AT2e).

Skills involved
Pupils will be:
- interpreting pictures to suggest meaning
- thinking about different ways of achieving harmony and co-existence
- finding out about two different religious projects aimed at creating peace.

Information
In the fourth activity pupils focus on an Interfaith Youth Council. There are many examples of interfaith groups which work on local, national and international level, such as the Interfaith Dialogue Network which was established in 1994 to provide a focus for interfaith dialogue. If the local area does not have a faith youth council or SACRE then a visiting speaker may be able to come to explain their aims and work to the pupils.

Use of ICT
Research: To use the Internet to find out more about Corrymeela or the Children of Abraham in the homework tasks.
Communication: In Activity 2 pupils could use ICT to produce the cartoon.
ICT Resource: See *Framework RE 3 ICT Resource* Teacher's Notes, page 103.

Activity 1 (AT2d)
The first activity develops pupils' use of visual literacy. By giving them a very rigid time limit, they have to focus on the main features of the picture. The picture is actually set in Jerusalem but pupils may refer to any areas where they think there would be Jews, Muslims and Christians. The picture shows a crescent to represent Islam, Magen David to represent Judaism and a cross to represent Christianity.

Activity 2 (AT1a and AT2b)
Worksheets 5.6 and 5.7
From their investigation of the information, pupils are asked to identify key features of the work of Corrymeela and Children of Abraham and to analyse the short- and long-term effects (they can use Worksheet 5.6 for this). Pupils may distinguish the different approaches that are used, for example, face-to-face meetings; photographs; chat-rooms. This will help support ideas for the 'Now try this' activity.

For some high ability pupils, Worksheet 5.7 should be used to develop pupils understanding of the importance of Abraham to Christianity, Islam and Judaism. It gives opportunity for a detailed analysis of the role of Abraham and the different interpretations given by Muslims and Jews.

Activity 3 (AT2b)
In the first part of the activity pupils will show an understanding of the aims of the Interfaith Youth Council and link them with the appropriate pictures. Answers could include:
Picture 1 – to develop self-confidence and increase understanding of those with beliefs different from their own.
Picture 2 – to promote understanding, respect and positive co-operation.
Picture 3 – to encourage the teenagers to work together to make decisions about their community.
The second part of the activity asks for a reasoned evaluation, which uses evidence either from this lesson or past learning. This can be done as a role-play exercise if it is considered appropriate.

Now try this (extension work) (AT2d and AT2e)
This extension activity requires pupils to use reasoning and insights into the challenges of belonging to a religion in the contemporary world. Pupils may mention:
- working with people of different faiths broadens your mind
- meeting people of different faiths helps you make friends and breakdown stereotypes and misconceptions you may have of people.

Pupils may refer to a number of reasons for 'closed minds', for example, lack of experiences, parental views, poor previous experiences.

Suggestions for homework and follow-up work

1 Research Corrymeela or Children of Abraham and produce a pamphlet that could be used with a Year 6 class explaining what each organisation does.
2 Pupils could set up a youth council within the school.

Framework RE 3 ICT Resource Teacher's Notes

Starter activity

This activity introduces pupils to key terms that will be used throughout the lesson. Pupils should flip over a card from each row to see if the words, pictures and definitions match. When they match the cards will disappear from the screen. This activity will support visual learners and includes some key concepts used in GCSE examinations.

Answers

1 Coexistence, picture d, living together peacefully.
2 Conflict, picture c, disagreements.
3 Harmony, picture b, being in agreement.
4 Dialogue, picture a, talking and listening to each other.

Main activity

This activity requires pupils to make a judgement and be able to justify it. After they have individually chosen and justified the order in which they would put the different ways that people can learn to live in harmony, the activity could be opened up to a class discussion where a consensus decision is made on the order. Alternatively you could create a class graph or pie chart showing how many of the class chose each way as the most successful and the least successful.

The answers are subjective but pupils should be able to justify their selections using specific evidence where possible.

Plenary activity

In this activity pupils can be divided into teams so that they negotiate a joint decision on which word or phrase is the odd one out. This means that pupils will have to justify their selections in an explanation to the group.

The answers are subjective and will depend upon pupils' depth of understanding. The important part of this activity is the process that pupils use to come to a justified decision.

There are four lists in total, one on each screen. Click on the arrow at the bottom of the screen to go on to the next.

Suggested answers

1 a) Abraham because he did not go with Hagar and Ishmael.
  b) Hagar because she was a woman.
2 a) Conflict because it is negative.
  b) Dialogue because it is the link between conflict and harmony.
3 a) Corrymeela because it is particularly involved with harmony within Christianity.
  b) Children of Abraham because the members do not usually see each other but work through ICT.
  c) Interfaith Youth Council because it has children from a range of different traditions.
4 a) Going to different places of worship as you will meet members of that religion.

5. WHAT ATTITUDES DO RELIGIONS HAVE TO FORGIVENESS?

Pupil's Book pages 112–115

Aim

The aim of the lesson is to investigate why many people consider it important to forgive.

Learning objectives

By the end of the lesson pupils should have:

- been able to discuss and express ideas about the qualities needed to forgive and to be forgiven (AT1f and 2c)
- analysed a range of sacred texts concerning forgiveness (AT1a and 1e)
- reflected on the importance of forgiving (AT2b)
- gained a knowledge and understanding of the importance of Yom Kippur for many Jews (AT1b).

Skills involved

Pupils will be:

- thinking about the power of forgiving
- considering the impact of beliefs on forgiveness
- finding out about the importance of Yom Kippur for many Jews.

Information

Dr Ken Hart, while at Leeds University, showed how forgiving people can improve people's health. His research showed that people suffered less from both physical and mental illness.

Terry Waite CBE was advisor to the Archbishop of Canterbury when he was taken hostage in Lebanon in 1987 for 1763 days. For the first four years he was kept in solitary confinement. One of his role models is Archbishop Desmond Tutu. He said:

'If one can understand why people behave as they do then often the road to forgiveness is opened. Not only is forgiveness essential for the health of society, it is also vital for our personal well-being. Bitterness is like a cancer that enters the soul. It does more harm to those that hold it than to those whom it is held against'.

Use of ICT

Research: To find out more about the 'f project' (www.theforgivenessproject.com) or the Tariq Khasima Foundation (www.tkf.org) for homework or follow-up activity.

Communication: To record findings and present them to others in the 'Now try this' activity.

ICT Resource: See *Framework RE 3 ICT Resource* Teacher's Notes, page 105.

Activity 1 (AT2c)

Pupils may consider a range of different reasons. Examples may include that it is:

- mind over matter
- the effect of reconciliation
- the release of any guilt
- taking on new interests.

There may be opportunities for pupils to reflect upon their own experiences of guilt although this should only be introduced if teachers consider it appropriate.

Activity 2 (AT1f, AT1a and AT2b)

Pupils are asked to make sense of the information and to consider the different pairs of emotions that the two main characters felt during the story. These pairs of emotions could be compared to the emotions in the Parable of the Forgiving Father. All pupils should be using a wide range of religious terms such as reconciliation, repentance and forgiveness. Pupils should identify what helped change one emotion to the other, for example, Azim felt despair when he heard how his son had died but, through the work of the Foundation, he has hope for the future.

In the second part of the activity pupils should use prior knowledge of Islam to answer the question. A wide range of justifications could be given, such as:

- it is what God wants
- it is considered a blessing from God
- the community of faith members would be a support
- a belief in after-life would help.

Activity 3 (AT1b and AT1e)   Worksheet 5.8

By investigating a range of sacred texts all pupils should be aware of the many ways that are given as examples for expressing forgiveness. The examples also show the active role that the person who has been wronged has. Answers may include:

- kissing their feet
- continuing to forgive
- forgetting
- going to their house
- not repaying with evil.

Worksheet 5.8 extends this activity by looking at Terrry Waite's forgiveness of his captors.

Now try this (extension work) (AT1a)

This activity can relate to any religious traditions. Pupils should be able to include a wide range of concepts to reflect the beliefs, values and traditions of faith communities. Examples of key concepts may include:

- teaching from sacred texts
- the worshipping community
- key beliefs, for example, life after death
- sources of authority in the tradition
- previous experiences.

Suggestions for homework and follow-up work

1 Compare the information about Tariq Khamisa to teachings found in sacred texts, for example, the Parable of the Forgiving Father (Christianity) and the Story of Angulimala (Buddhism).
2 Research more about the Tariq Khasima Foundation.

Framework RE 3 ICT Resource Teacher's Notes

Starter activity

This activity gives pupils an opportunity for peer discussion. The discussion will support Activity Two and Activity Three in the Pupil's Book (pages 113 and 114). Pupils' should be encouraged to explore concepts such as motive, atonement and repentance in their explanations.

There are three statements in total, one on each screen. Click on the arrow at the bottom of the screen to go on to the next.

Main activity

When 'start' is clicked on the screen will show the picture of the Rosh Hashanah card for one minute. Then the picture will disappear and pupils should collaborate in small groups to draw or name what they saw and explain why these items are on the card. It is important that pupils use the correct religious terminology.

The picture will be replaced by the inside of the card. After they have completed the first part of the activity pupils should discuss in groups what the message should be, then come up and write their message in the card.

Answers
The card shows:

- shofar (used throughout the festival to call people to examine their lives)
- two candles (traditionally used to welcome in a festival)
- New Year greetings
- grapes (to signify a sweet New Year).

Plenary activity

As this lesson in the Pupil's Book (pages 112–115) includes many personal stories it is important that pupils can recognise that these are illustrations of the main teaching points. This activity should focus pupils on the main teachings of the lesson.

Suggested answers
Summary points pupils should come up with include:

- the importance of being able to forgive and how this can improve someone's health
- the relationship between the forgiver and the forgiven
- ways that people can forgive
- forgiveness within religious traditions
- when might be the right time to forgive
- the role of teshuvah – repentance
- Yom Kippur.

6. WHEN MIGHT CONFLICT BE NECESSARY?

Pupil's Book pages 116–119

Aim

The aim of this lesson is to give pupils opportunities to consider if it is right to cause conflict for the protection of human rights.

Learning objectives

By the end of the lesson pupils should have:
- explained why some people consider it important to stand up for the rights of others (AT2e)
- discussed what issues they consider are important to stand up for (AT2f)
- understood the impact of the beliefs and actions of Chiune Sugihara and Rosa Parks (AT2d).

Skills involved

Pupils will be:
- discussing how responsible we should be for protecting human rights
- analysing the impact of Rosa Parks's and Chiune Sugihara's beliefs on their actions
- thinking about what they might make a stand for.

Information

The case studies are presented in two different forms. There is further information available through the use of search-engines.

Chiune and his wife Yukiko Sugihara were diplomats in Lithuania when the Second World War broke out. Chiune Sugihara was born in Japan in 1900. He joined the Foreign Ministry, and in 1938 he was posted to the Japanese diplomatic office in Finland and then sent in 1939 to Lithuania. Six months later war broke out and the Soviets ordered all consulates to be closed. It was during this time that he received thousands of requests from Polish Jews who were fleeing Poland. The refugees realised that the only way out of the country was to flee east and needed visas to get through Japan. So Sugihara had a dilemma to obey either his government or his conscience. (He had during his life converted to become a Russian Orthodox.) He said: 'human life is very important, and being virtuous in life is important as well'. From 31 July to 28 August 1940, Mr and Mrs Sugihara signed over 300 visas a day.

After the war he never spoke about his deed but in 1969 some of the people he had helped escape asked for him to be honoured in Yad Vashem – the Holocaust Memorial in Israel where a tree was planted and a park named in his honour.

Rosa Parks was riding home on a bus after work in Montgomery on 1 December 1955. She quietly refused to give up her seat on the bus and was arrested. The law in Alabama segregated black and white people. There were separate entrances to shops, separate park benches, etc. Her action sparked many people into action. A few days later thousands of people met at the local Baptist Church and agreed to boycott the buses. The minister was Martin Luther King. Rosa Parks died on 24 October 2005.

Use of ICT

Research: To use Internet search facilities to find further information concerning Rosa Parks and Chiune Sugihara (www.rosaparks.org and www.rongreene.com/sugihara).
Communication: In Activity 2 pupils could present their film plan using ICT.
ICT Resource: See *Framework RE 3 ICT Resource Teacher's Notes*, page 107.

Activity 1 (AT2e) Worksheet 5.9

Before completing the activity pupils could complete Worksheet 5.9 to develop their knowledge and understanding of human rights. The purpose of this activity is for the pupils to consider what human rights issues are particularly important for them.

From the dialogue and poem, pupils may identify reasons for standing up for others, for example:
- as human beings, we should care for all
- if people don't stand up, the result could be more genocides
- people who discriminate often base their views on stereotypes
- causes may be just
- there are no other ways.

Activity 2 (AT2c)

Pupils are asked to present their knowledge and understanding of the actions of Rosa Parks. In the first part of the activity pupils express their knowledge and understanding concerning the motivation and challenges to Rosa Park's actions through creating a plan for a film of her life.

An important aspect of the second part of the activity is for pupils to understand the long-term impacts of the stand that Rosa Parks made and a consideration of the long-term legacy.

Activity 3 (AT1/2)

In the third part of the activity, pupils may relate their answer to the peace cranes created by Sadako in Lesson 3. The fourth part of the activity requires pupils to engage with information and to consider a range of related questions and tasks. When pupils are considering the description on the plaque they may refer to the fact that

Chiune Sugihara did this at a cost to himself, or that through one action had an impact on the lives of so many.

Now try this (extension work) (AT2d)

When pupils complete the Venn diagram they will be able to distinguish many similarities and differences.

Similarities include:

- Both Chiune's and Rosa's actions had a considerable effect on many people.
- Both were punished for their actions.
- Both used non-violent methods of conflict.

Differences include:

- Chiune's did not profit him at all.
- Chiune's actions were taken over a long period of time.

Suggestions for homework and follow-up work

Investigate further the life of Rosa Parks and Chiune Sugihara.

Framework RE 3 ICT Resource Teacher's Notes

Starter activity

Pupils should try to think of the connection between each picture and taking a stand or making a difference. All the pictures and issues have been previously introduced in the Pupil's Book. If pupils need prompts they can click on the card again for suggested answers.

There are seven pictures in total, one on each screen. Click on the arrow at the bottom of the screen to go on to the next.

Suggested answers

1 Muhammad Ali refused to fight in the Vietnam War.
2 Matthew and Karina Archer set up a shelter for homeless children in Brazil.
3 Bob Geldof speaks out to put pressure on political leaders to solve the problem of poverty in Africa.
4 Anita Roddick used business ethics to promote social and environmental change.
5 Nkosi Johnson publicised the importance of supporting people with AIDS.
6 Peace cranes were originally made to promote peace.
7 Azim Khamisa forgave the killer of his son.

Main activity

There are two parts to this activity. Pupils are asked to sequence five events in the life of Rosa Parks by dragging and dropping the pictures into the correct order. This will help pupils with Activity Two in the Pupil's Book (page 117). On the next screen they are asked to sequence five events in Sugihara's life. Some pupils might consider corresponding emotions that are appropriate for each picture. Click on the arrow at the bottom of the screen to go on to the next.

Answers
Rosa Parks

1 Segregation on a bus in America.
2 Rosa refuses to move on the bus.
3 The police arrive to arrest Rosa.
4 A virtually empty bus; people walking.
5 Bus with black and white passengers sitting next to each other.

Chiune Sugihara

1 The German invasion.
2 Jews line up outside Sugihara's door.
3 Telegram sent from Japan refusing the issue of visas.
4 The Sugiharas write many visas.
5 Sugihara has to resign for disobeying orders.

Plenary activity

Pupils are asked to complete a short piece of writing. They should be able to recognise what the visit/pilgrimage would mean and describe what they did on their visit. Pupils may refer to the importance of the paper cranes.

FRAMEWORK RE 3
Worksheet 5.1

Use this worksheet to help you with Activity Three.

Task

Put a tick next to each statement that you believe would be a just war.

1. The last resort – all the non-violent options have been explored. ▢

2. A country doesn't like the fact there is more oil in another country. ▢

3. A person says three times 'let's have a war'. ▢

4. It is started and controlled by the government ▢

5. There is a possibility of winning the war. ▢

6. Hospitals and schools are the first targets to be bombed. ▢

7. Every effort is made not to kill innocent people. ▢

8. At the end of the war the good achieved will outweigh the loss. ▢

9. People vote to go to war. ▢

10. To defend your religion. ▢

Do you think you can have rules in a war?

Fill in the template below.

I think that _____

_____

The reason I think this is because _____

_____

However, some people such as _____ think that_____

_____

_____

FRAMEWORK RE 3

Worksheet 5.2

Use this worksheet to help you with Activity Two.

FRAMEWORK RE 3

Worksheet 5.3

Use this worksheet to help you with Activity Three.

Task

Complete the triangle to answer the question 'Should Christians go to war?'.

In the second layer of the triangle add factors which might influence their decision (for example, 'Conscience') and in the bottom layer of the triangle expand on these factors with more detail or evidence (for example, 'Is it right to kill another human being?').

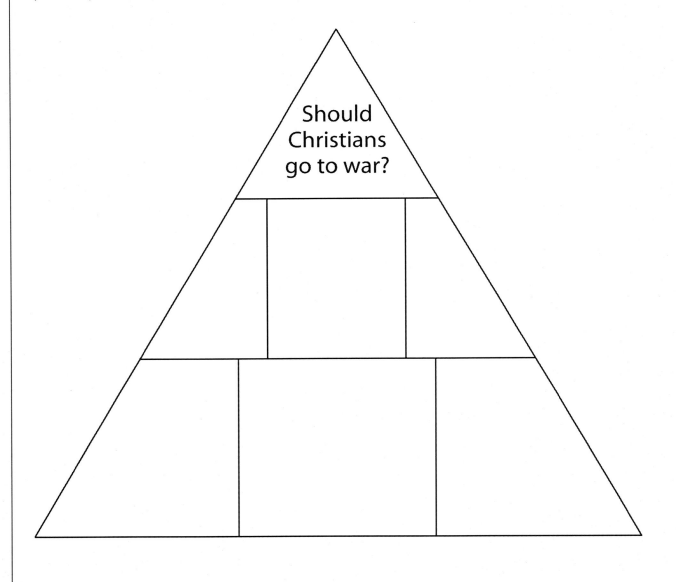

Should Christians go to war?

FRAMEWORK RE 3

Worksheet 5.4

Use this worksheet to help you with Activities One and Two.

Task

1.   There are many different attitudes to peace. Read through the quotes and highlight those you agree with.

2.   If you had to choose an inspirational quote for your selected project which would you choose and why?

'Peace is better than war because in peace the sons bury their fathers, but in war fathers bury their sons.'
Croesus – King of Lydia (from Greek mythology)

'Blessed are the Peacemakers.'
St Matthew – The Bible

'I am an absolute pacifist … it is an instinctive feeling. It is a feeling that possesses me because the murder of men is disgusting.'
Albert Einstein – scientist

'Peace is not just the absence of war … Like a cathedral, peace must be constructed patiently and with unshakable faith.'
Pope John Paul II

'Peace is a journey of a thousand miles and it must be taken one step at a time.'
Lyndon B. Johnson – former US president

'Peace is a state of mind, not a state of the nation.'
Marilyn Ferguson – poet

'Peace is not the product of terror or fear.
Peace is not the silence of cemeteries.
Peace is not the silent result of violent oppression.
Peace is the generous, tranquil contribution of all to the good of all.
Peace is dynamism. Peace is generosity.
It is right and duty.'
Oscar Romero – priest

'Nothing can bring you peace but yourself.'
Ralph Waldo Emerson – philosopher

'If you want to make peace with your enemy you have to work with your enemy – then they become your partner.'
Nelson Mandela

FRAMEWORK RE 3

Worksheet 5.5

Use this worksheet to help you with Activity Two.

Peace Project Justification

Name:
Aim: To establish a project for the community to work together.
1. How was the project used elsewhere?
2. How did the project involve people from the community?
3. How will it have a lasting effect?
4. Which quote would you use for your project (from Worksheet 5.4)?   Explain your choice.

FRAMEWORK RE 3

Worksheet 5.6

Use this worksheet to help you with Activity Two.

Result
Long-term

Action

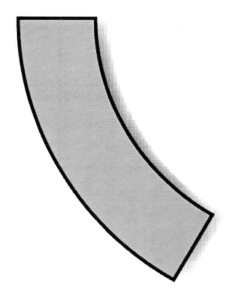

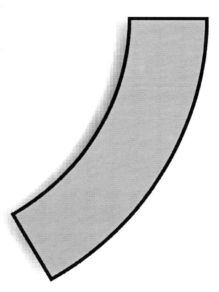

Result
Short-term

FRAMEWORK RE 3

Worksheet 5.7

Use this worksheet to help you with Activity Two.

Task

Abraham is an important person for Jews and Muslims. Below, a Jew and a Muslim retell the story from their own tradition.

- In yellow highlighter, highlight the many similarities between the two stories.

- In a blue highlighter, highlight any features which are distinct to the Jewish source.

- In a green highlighter, highlight any features which are distinct to the Muslim source.

Jewish source

Abram lived in the country we now call Iraq. He loved God and tried to get people to stop worshipping the other gods. For this he was persecuted and so he and his wife, Sarai, left to go to Egypt. The King of Egypt asked Hagar, an Egyptian lady, to go with Abram and Sarai. Many years passed and still Abram had no children and he was more than 80 years old. Sarai told him to marry Hagar. Soon they had a child called Ishmael. When Abram was 99 he was told by God to change his name from Abram ('exalted father') to Abraham ('Father of Nations') and Sarai was to change her name to Sarah and that she would bear a son called Isaac. The Lord said he would bless both Isaac and Ishmael and both their descendents would become great nations.

Sarah went on to have a baby called Isaac but was upset by Hagar and Ishmael and wanted them to go. So Abraham took Hagar and Ishmael out in the desert but soon they had no water. God saw their distress and provided a well for them to drink from.

Later God tested Abraham by ordering him to sacrifice Isaac. Just as the sacrifice was about to happen God said 'Stop' and told Abraham to sacrifice a ram that had been caught in the bushes instead.

FRAMEWORK RE 3
Worksheet 5.7 (continued)

Muslim source

Prophet Ibrahim lived in the country we now call Iraq. He loved Allah and tried to get people to stop worshipping the other gods. For this he was persecuted and so he and his wife, Sarah, left to go to Egypt.

Allah gave him the good news that he was to have a son who would be a prophet. The King of Egypt asked Hajar, an Egyptian lady, to be with Prophet Ibrahim and Sarah. Many years passed and still Prophet Ibrahim had no children. Sarah told him to marry Hajar so that they may have a child. Soon they had a baby they called Ismail. Shortly after Prophet Ibrahim told Hajar that the Lord had told him to take her to a place called Makkah and leave her alone there. He did not understand why he had to do this but obeyed.

Soon after he had left Hajar and Ismail, their water was gone. Hajar ran between the hills of Marwah and Safa praying to Allah for help. Right beside the baby water flowed from the ground. The water is still flowing today and is called Zam-zam.

Many years later Prophet Ibrahim returned to Makkah and found Hajar and Ismail. He dreamt in Makkah that Allah ordered him to sacrifice Ismail. The Prophet told Ismail what he had dreamt and they both wanted to obey Allah. Just as the sacrifice was to happen Allah said 'Stop' and told Prophet Ibrahim to sacrifice a lamb instead. When Prophet Ibrahim returned to Palestine the angel of Allah told him that he was to have another son called Ishaq with his first wife Sarah.

FRAMEWORK RE 3

Worksheet 5.8

Use this worksheet to help you with Activity Three.

Terry Waite was held hostage for a number of years in Lebanon. After his release he was asked how he felt about his captors. He replied:

'Bitterness is like a cancer that enters the soul. It does more harm to those that hold it than to those whom it is held against.'

Task

Write a response using the support framework below. In your answer include at least three of the following words:

- reconciliation
- guilt
- blessing
- compassion
- repentance
- revenge

1. I think Terry Waite was saying that …
2. I agree /disagree because …   An example would be when …
3. I also agree/disagree because …   This was seen when …
However I can see people would disagree with me because …

FRAMEWORK RE 3

Worksheet 5.8 (continued)

The examples in the Pupil's Book on page 114 and these additional examples should help you.

> A former inmate of a Nazi concentration camp was visiting a friend who had shared the ordeal with him.
>
> 'Have you forgiven the Nazis?' he asked his friend
>
> 'Yes.'
>
> 'Well I haven't. I'm still consumed with hatred for them.'
>
> 'In that case' said his friend gently 'they still have you in prison'
>
> De Mello, *Heart of the Enlightened*

> Jill Saward was raped in a vicarage in West London when she was 18, and her father Canon Michael Saward and boyfriend were seriously injured. She said:
>
> 'I hated what they had done to me and my family but I did not hate them. I have seen so many people destroyed by not being able to move on. Hating becomes a form of self-protection.'

> Lesley Blinda's husband was working for a Christian relief agency called Tearfund when he was murdered in Rwanda. She decided it was important to go to the prison were the murderers were and to forgive them face to face.

> Betty Ferguson's daughter was murdered. She drank a lot, neglected her other four children and continually wanted to get even with her daughter's murderer Ray Payne who had been her daughter's English teacher. She says, 'I was consumed with hatred.' When her sister died she went to the funeral and heard one of the lines from the Lord's Prayer:
>
> 'Forgive those who trespass against us'.
>
> She began to say like a mantra 'I am willing to forgive Ray' and after a few months she wrote to him and then went to visit him. She explained to him what the loss of her daughter had meant while he listened in silence and then they both broke down and cried. As she left she felt a very different person. She says 'forgiveness is the greatest gift I gave myself.'

FRAMEWORK RE 3

Worksheet 5.9

Use this worksheet to help you with Activity One.

So what rights would you stand up for?

The UN Convention on the Rights of the Child lays down the rights of all children under the age of 18 years.
1. Read the rights below.
2. In groups, identify which are most important, quite important or not very important.
3. Select one which you would consider most important and how, in the way you live your life, you could show it.

RIGHTS	MOST IMPORTANT	QUITE IMPORTANT	NOT IMPORTANT
Right to a birth certificate			
Children shouldn't be separated from parents unless it is for their own good			
If parents live apart, children have the right to stay in contact with both parents			
Children should be protected from violence			
Children should not be allowed to do work that is dangerous			
No child should be punished in a way that humiliates them			
Children have a right to meet others and make friends			
Children have a right to think and believe what they want and to practice their religion			
Parents should help children to learn between right and wrong			
Children have a right to an education			
Children have the right to relax and play			
Children have a right to live			
Children who are disabled have a right to special care			
Children under 16 should not take a direct part in any conflict			
Children who have suffered in any way have a right to get help in a safe place to help them recover			